COACHING CAREERS AND PERFORMANCE

■ ■ ■

THE MANAGEMENT GUIDE
TO SUPPORTING
YOUR EMPLOYEES'
CAREER DEVELOPMENT
AND PERFORMANCE

GERALD M. STURMAN Ph.D.

BIERMAN HOUSE, INC. • BEDFORD, NY

Coaching Careers and Performance

Fourth Edition
©2000 Bierman House, Inc.
19 Brookwood Road
Bedford, NY 10506
(914) 234-3200

ISBN 0-9626887-2-X

Contents

Preface

You Depend on Your Employees

As a manager or supervisor you have a lot of responsibility. You have your own work to do, in addition to managing and supervising others. The work of the people who report to you must meet your standards and support your work mission. You have to report to your own manager and meet his or her standards. The effectiveness of your own work, and along with it, your reputation, salary, and career depend on how well those who report to you get their work done. In the ideal world, your employees would always perform at their peak, keep developing themselves to expand their ability to contribute, and never have attitude or behavior problems. Unfortunately, these ideal conditions are seldom, if ever, met. Every day, you confront the task of keeping the people around you working efficiently, effectively, purposefully, and productively. You can appreciate that if you got really good at doing this part of your job, it would probably make your whole worklife easier and more joyful.

How can you move toward the ideal? What is the most effective way of handling this part of the management job? How can you motivate and support people to be productive, to keep developing themselves and to reduce or eliminate negative or ineffective attitudes and behaviors? And — how can you do all this with a minimum of time and energy?

The Rewards Are Worth the Effort

The purpose of this handbook is to support you, as a manager, to master the skill of coaching your employees in performance and career development. We recognize that your scarcest resource is your own time. The idea here is to make your work and life easier. Becoming an effective coach will take some practice on your part, but the rewards will be significant and far greater than the cost of time and energy spent.

The Courage to Coach

It takes courage to coach! You will sometimes have to confront an employee whose performance or behavior is unacceptable. This confrontation can be uncomfortable, embarrassing, or even frightening. You might want to avoid the issue and live with the consequences rather than face the discomfort. Or you may try to push the problem over to someone else — human resources, for example. Sometimes, you might find it easier to fire someone than to coach them toward meeting standards. Coaching someone with whom you are having difficulty takes a commitment to the individual and his or her development. You will need to remember that

v

your employees are human beings with the potential to grow and change and give their best. You will need to recognize this potential when things are not going well. You will need to set aside your own immediate agenda to be able to hear your employee's side of the story. You will need to be open, and compassionate, and firm at the same time. You will need to uphold a standard that may be difficult for the employee to meet. You will need to balance your impatience for short-term results with the rewards of long-term individual development. You will need to examine your own needs for power and control in the light of ensuring that the job gets done, not only today, but over the long haul. In short — you will need to summon the courage to coach.

Thanks to Those Who Contributed

Much of the material in this book was developed by W. Breese White when he was Vice President for Training and Development for The Career Development Team. His work and his commitment to the thousands of people who participated in the workshops he led is gratefully acknowledged.

The work of Mitzi Gregory, Mary Crannell, Lorrie Appleton, and Nettie Spiwack in the ongoing delivery and development of this material in workshops is also gratefully acknowledged.

I wish to thank Peggy C. Bier, President of The Career Development Team for her leadership and continuing commitment to high quality in all of the work we do together.

We are also grateful to the many fine organizations and people around the country who have shared their worklives with us and taught us the lessons we share with you in this handbook.

Gerald M. Sturman
Bedford, NY
October, 1992

Why Is Coaching Important...?

Welcome

Welcome to Coaching Careers and Performance!

The purpose of this Handbook is:

> *To enhance your ability to be effective in supporting your employees in managing their performance and their careers.*

Forging the Relationship

The essential part of the relationship between you and the people who work for you has to do with their perfomance and their careers. It is important for you to forge your relationship around both of these critical elements in the individual's worklife.

Each individual's career is a personal, lifelong quest for satisfaction and accomplishment, for learning and growth, for the security of reasonable income appropriate to contribution, and for an important form of self-expression.

Careers Can Be Frustrating

The ideals that people hold in relation to their careers are not easily matched by the reality of their jobs. Sometimes they are frustrated or even angry.

The principal cause of this anger and frustration is not only the disparity between the ideal and reality, but the sense that nothing can really be done about it — the disempowerment that can come from being the *little individual* in the big corporation.

Opportunity

Coaching provides the opportunity for you you contribute to the well-being, satisfaction and effectiveness of your employees by supporting them in this important aspect of their lives. It leads to enhanced productivity, better team work, and on a more personal level, a strong reputation for you as someone who cares about the people who work for you and supports their personal development. This opportunity is available, easy to fulfill, and enormously satisfying for you as well as for your employees. It can also be great fun!

Fundamental Issues

The performance of your employees has a direct impact on you and your ability to meet the goals for which *you* are accountable. Coaching people in the process of managing their careers may not be as obvious. Career management deals with the fundamental issues in the work lives of your employees — issues that deal with the very nature of who they are as human beings — their hopes, dreams, ambitions, and, sometimes even their survival.

Satisfaction and Performance

To the extent that they are satisfied in their work lives, many people are satisfied in the rest of their lives. Satisfaction is also associated with improved performance. If satisfaction can be enhanced through proper attention to an employee's career, it may be possible to improve performance. For this reason alone, it may be important to provide appropriate opportunity for your employees to give attention to the development of their careers.

Individual Contribution and Organizational Success

There is an even more important reason! As you will see in the following section, career management has to do with more than individual success and satisfaction. The true context of career management has to do with the contribution of the individual to the success of the organization.

By supporting your employees' career management you will be directly supporting their contributions to the organization.

Win-Win

When your employees expand their contribution to the organization (your division, or department, or group, or work team), they expand your ability to get your job done and meet your own goals. In this sense, their development is your development!

Effective Investment

Career management is difficult for employees to do effectively without the support and guidance of a coach — particularly and most importantly their managers or supervisors. Providing this support can be one of the most important elements of your job as a manager, and can contribute to the success of you and your organization. The investment in time and effort is small in comparison with the potential benefits in employee satisfaction, effectiveness, and long-term ability to get the job done with excellence.

Within this framework it becomes clear that future possibilities are based on an individual's ability to perform his or her current functions at an acceptable level.

The Link

This is the link between the present and the future. Your feedback and attention to employee performance, not just at review time but throughout the year, combined with regular interactions around the management of their careers forms a strong foundation for fulfilling potential and enhancing job satisfaction.

Career Coaching and Performance Coaching: The Distinction

The Distinction

While performance and career management are definitely linked, your role in coaching these areas is different and distinct. Understanding this distinction, and coaching consistent with the distinction, can allow you to be more comfortable and confident in your interaction with your employees.

Performance: Black or White

In the performance coaching session, your role is to take a position regarding the employee, provide the specific evidence that validates your assessment, offer actions relative to improvement, and then follow up. Your position is a black or white stance. Either the standards of performance for the job were met or not. There should be no gray in interpreting the individual's results.

Careers: Non-positional

In a career coaching session you need to be non-positional. The career meeting needs to be a safe place for employees to bring up any issues they have around their careers and to be supported in taking the next step which will move them closer to their goals. Non-positional doesn't mean that you don't have an opinion or point of view regarding their plans or goals. You have a valuable opinon which is important for your employee to receive, but you can't be attached to what they do with your input.

Your Investment

Your investment in these two interactions is also distinct. You are definitely invested in the results of a performance discussion. You want the performance to improve! Your investment in the results of your career conversations is not the same. You want your employees to take responsibility for what they do with your input, support and suggestions — not that they have to do what you say. The choice is theirs.

Enhanced Personal Satisfaction

Effective career and performance coaching can give you enormous personal satisfaction and a reputation as a manager who supports, encourages, and develops your people. This reputation enhances the possibility for you in your own career and creates a pulling effect for people to want to work for you.

Your straight talk and interaction around performance allows people to grow and deal with their personal responsibility for the results they produce and their development toward expanding their contribution to the organization.

The Fundamentals Of Career and Performance Management

The Meaning of Work

Work, in its deepest and most personal meaning is *"…the expression of Self in the contribution of value."* People derive satisfaction from their work by making a contribution appropriate to their own abilities and desires and useful to their organizations. The deepest satisfaction comes from doing that work as effectively as possible. Only the individual can be truly responsible for discovering his or her own desires and best abilities and seek ways to use these to make the maximum contribution to the goals of the organization. True work satisfaction lies in the full realization of this responsibility.

Career and Performance Management

"Career and performance management is the process in which employees take responsibility for developing their ability to make an expanded contribution to the organization…a contribution linking individual work satisfaction and performance to the goals and challenges of the organization."

Career and performance management is not, therefore, about "getting ahead." It is, rather, about getting to be the best you can be and expressing your excellence in contributing to the goals of your organization. People discover the opportunity for expanded contribution by looking at their current job with the renewed perspective of effective career management. This leads to the recognition for enhancing performance. A strong foundation in what true career management means validates the performance discussion.

The Challenge of Change

All across America, in organizations large and small, the same thing is heard — in today's workworld and economy, individuals must prepare themselves for rapid changes by being aware of their abilities and by being flexible and adaptable to different needs in their industries that are yet unforeseen.

Mutually Supportive Process of Discovery

More and more organizations are providing a supportive environment for their employees to discover themselves and their most contributive role. In this mutually supportive process of discovery, which we call *career management*, lies the future success of organizations and the people who create them.

Notes

What Is A Good Coach...?

The Manager's Role

One of your key roles as a manager is to coach your employees. You have a team of individuals with unique contributions to make and diverse goals and needs. Your job is to be able to support and direct each person toward the realization of his or her particular needs and goals while ensuring the fulfillment of the team's objectives. A professional career counselor — no. An effective coach — yes!

Coach

COACH — "...one who instructs or trains a performer."
TRAIN — "...to aim at an object or objective."

Coaching is a partnership in which it is possible to realize mutual potential. A coach is *not* necessarily a better player. A coach is *not* someone who invalidates because they think they know better. Effective coaching requires the suspension of existing assumptions, judgements, and beliefs about the individual so that you can guide them toward their aspirations.

A Good Coach

The qualities and skills of being a good coach parallel those of a good manager. A good coach is someone who is able:

- to listen and discover where people are stuck and what support they need to be able to move on;

- to observe from outside the game and see things that the players themselves may not;

- to have the larger view and provide information and advice to support the players;

- to discern the needs and goals of each person and know that each one needs different direction to support his or her development.

A good coach not only has these skills but is able to use them to enhance individual performance. All of this occurs in the partnership between the player and the coach. In the area of performance and careers, your employees are the players and you are the coach.

A good coach recognizes the individuality of each team member and is there to provide the guidance and direction to allow each individual to be the responsible player in his or her own career. To fulfill this role the coach must be honest, encouraging, direct, responsive, supportive, and must develop a partnership with the players.

A Good Coach Is Someone Who...

- **Guides and enhances our ability to observe, clarify, and discern.**

- **Shows us the possibility of realizing our potential.**

- **Reveals the mastery of a technique.**

Your Current Coaching Skills

Are You Meeting Your Own Standards?

Test your ability to be an effective coach and discover where you can make some needed improvements. Check your answer to each of the questions as honestly and as objectively as possible.

As a manager, I (Seldom, Sometimes, Often):

	SELDOM	SOMETIMES	OFTEN
1. Listen carefully to what employees have to say…	_____	_____	_____
2. Acknowledge employees when they have accomplished something, even if it seems like a small win…	_____	_____	_____
3. Keep up-to-date about what's going on in the company so I can provide useful information to my employees…	_____	_____	_____
4. Avoid gossiping about my employees and maintain confidentiality in my discussions with them and about them…	_____	_____	_____
5. Set clear standards of performance and communicate them clearly and as often as necessary…	_____	_____	_____
6. Work and act in a way that sets an appropriate and strong example to my employees…	_____	_____	_____
7. Avoid negative comments about the company except when presenting solutions to someone who can do something about it…	_____	_____	_____
8. Earn trust rather than demand it…	_____	_____	_____

As a manager, I (Seldom, Sometimes, Often):

	SELDOM	SOMETIMES	OFTEN
9. Am willing to confront unpleasant issues when I need to…	_____	_____	_____
10. Keep current about available training and educational opportunities…	_____	_____	_____
11. Am willing to make time for my employees even when I am extremely busy…	_____	_____	_____
12. Provide performance feedback as frequently as necessary…	_____	_____	_____
13. Seek to find out what may be troubling an employee whose behavior or attitude suddenly changes…	_____	_____	_____
14. Take a real interest in the personal and career growth of my employees…	_____	_____	_____
15. Continue coaching employees through difficult times — for me, for them, or for the company…	_____	_____	_____
16. Look for what works best about an individual and try to support that…	_____	_____	_____
17. Know when to say… *"I don't know…"*	_____	_____	_____
18. Support self-esteem of those around me and avoid putting people down…	_____	_____	_____
19. Reach out to employees rather than always wait for them to come to me…	_____	_____	_____
20. Feel comfortable coaching…	_____	_____	_____

As a manager, I (Seldom, Sometimes, Often):

	SELDOM	SOMETIMES	OFTEN
21. Encourage appropriate risk-taking...	____	____	____
22. Maintain my sense of humor...	____	____	____
23. Support my employees to network and increase their visibility...	____	____	____
24. Avoid allowing personal prejudice to stand in the way of maintaining a supportive role...	____	____	____
25. Avoid all forms of sexual harassment and maintain vigilance for myself and others...	____	____	____
26. Encourage individual responsibility for career and performance management...	____	____	____
27. Seek professional help when a situation requires it...	____	____	____
28. Know when to say *"No"*...	____	____	____
29. Am willing to take risks in order to develop people...	____	____	____
30. Would let a good person leave if I thought it was in their best interest...	____	____	____
31. Keep current in my industry and share my knowledge with others...	____	____	____
32. Give new employees reasonable training and time to learn...	____	____	____
33. Committed to my own growth as a manager...	____	____	____

As a manager, I (Seldom, Sometimes, Often):

	SELDOM	SOMETIMES	OFTEN

34. Avoid all forms of discrimination and maintain vigilance for myself and others… _____ _____ _____

35. Confront disruptive behavior quickly and decisively… _____ _____ _____

36. Do formal performance appraisal at least annually… _____ _____ _____

37. Discuss career goals and development with each employee at least annually… _____ _____ _____

38. Consider it more important to be effective than to be well-liked or popular… _____ _____ _____

39. Have my own career plan, keep it current, and work to implement the actions… _____ _____ _____

40. Provide a proper environment for performance or career development meetings with my employees… _____ _____ _____

Go back over the assessment you just completed and select up to five behaviors where you checked *Seldom* that you would like to modify. Write them in the spaces below.

Behaviors I would like to modify:

1._____

2._____

3._____

4._____

5._____

Reality Check

The Appendix contains a form that you can photocopy and distribute to any of your employees from whom you would like to get feedback on your coaching skills. The form contains the same assessment you just completed. Feedback from your employees will provide a good reality check for you. You may want to revise the list you created at the bottom of the previous page after you receive the feedback.

Blocks to Being an Effective Coach

What Stops Us From Being Effective?

In order to be effective as a coach it is important to discover what it is that may be stopping you or getting in the way. These blocks generally fall into one of three categories. We call these categories the "DAM" that is blocking your ability to be an effective coach.

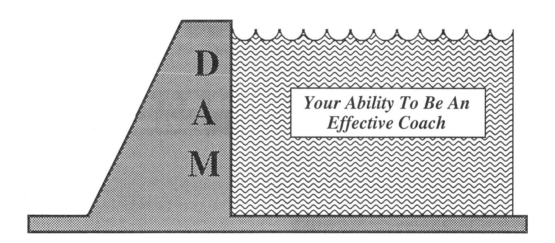

"DAM"

Deficiencies... Real or imagined..knowledge, skills, experience

Attributions... About you, others, the organization

Motivation...   Your own, others

Most of what blocks us falls into these areas, the foundation of which is motivation. Once motivated it is much easier to deal with the other blocks. If there is no motivation, there is no drive to handle the others.

Motivation

The motivation for both you and your employees lies in the definition of career management. The aim of career management, as we have defined it, is enhanced productivity, expanded contribution, and individual work satisfaction. Thus, both the organization and the individual profit. Your motivation should come from having the organizational view and wanting productivity increased, while the employees' motivation comes from a desire to have their work lives be satisfying and to make an expanded contribution.

Attributions

Once the motivation block is dealt with, the next major area of blockage lies in the labels or characterizations which we have of either ourselves, others, or the organization. These labels either "open" or "limit" what's possible. Since we have a natural tendency to label people, it is best to label in a way which can "open" possibilities.

Example: Jane is Bob's manager and needs to coach him in his career. Jane labels Bob as someone who "does poor work." When Bob discusses his goal of a promotion, Jane already has the possibility limited by the label. What is the evidence for the label? Jane says that Bob's reports always have misspellings and are always late. A new label that Jane could use that would "open" possibility is, "Bob is a poor speller and misses deadlines". Bob can't do anything about "does poor work." He can, however, deal directly with "poor speller and misses deadlines". Looking at the evidence provides information which "opens" possibilities for development.

Deficiencies

Your deficiencies are either real or imagined and fall into three areas: *skills, knowledge,* and *experience.* You get the experience by jumping in and engaging in the discussion with your employees. You don't need to know everything. Supporting your employees in finding out for themselves, and being able to direct them is the real job of a coach. As you practice coaching your skills will develop. As any good coach will tell you — practice, practice, practice.

The Career Management Process: AIM...CM

To support you in working with the diverse needs of employees and to promote individual responsibility, we have identified the five elements of the career management process. Use these five elements as a guide during your career management meeting with an employee. The elements are not to be followed rigidly — use them in a way that works for you and provides support to employees who may be stuck in the process.

AIM...CM

Assess

The career management process begins with employees learning as much about themselves as possible. What is their overall vision of their worklife and their contribution to the company. What skills have they developed that are useful to the organization? What is it that excites them and that they enjoy doing? What qualities do they possess? What is their style of work? What are their strengths, weaknesses, and shortcomings? There are many tools available to support people in this process all the way from sophisticated assessment systems to "do-it-yourself" books. Some of these tools are described later in this handbook.

Investigate

The second element involves research. Has the person investigated and discovered what the needs, challenges and opportunities are in the company, department, or division?

Match

Have they matched their particular assessment of themselves with the needs, challenges and opportunities? Is there a match?

Choose

Given their assessment and research, and having found a match, have they chosen appropriate development targets of opportunity? These targets should be both short term (on the current job) and long term. Targets may be either positional (including lateral moves) or skill development.

Manage

Have they created and implemented a plan with specific actions and deadlines? The plan could include skills to develop, experience to gain, behavior and attitudes to modify, and support to enlist.

The Five Elements of Effective Career Management

Has Your Employee:

AIM...CM

Assessed...	Style, motivation, skills, interests, qualities, experience, strengths, weaknesses and shortcomings, overall vision of worklife and contribution?
Investigated...	Needs, challenges, opportunities?
Matched...	Assessments with needs, challenges, opportunities?
Chosen...	Development targets of opportunity?
Managed...	Created and implemented a plan with action steps...skills to develop, behaviors and attitudes to improve, goals, support to develop?

The Performance Coaching Process: IMPROVER

Fundamental Rule

The fundamental rule in performance coaching is that the standards must be specific, clear, and agreed upon. Once the standards are established you have the playing field and rules defined. To support you we have developed the process presented below. Use this step-by-step approach as a guide in dealing with performance issues.

Identify the Need

The first step is to identify the need. What is the motivation to discuss performance? Is there a performance problem? Is it more appropriate to handle this in a career coaching session? Be specific in assessing the need.

Map Your Strategy

The second step involves your approach. Your strategy might include formal training, co-worker instruction, job restructuring, reassignment, etc.

Plan Your Coaching

Plan for your participation and for a meeting with the employee. How much time will you spend? How will progress be observed by you? What measures will you use for showing improvement?

Recommend the Actions

Meet with the employee. Present the situation and the facts. Allow the full expression of views, feelings, and concerns. Describe the strategy, plan, and recommended actions.

Obtain Agreement

Gain the employee's agreement on the strategy, plan, and recommended actions. Make sure any consequences are understood. Agreement is crucial.

View Their Performance

You must observe the employee's performance personally in order to be able to evaluate and coach appropriate to the plan and actions.

Evaluate

Using the agreed upon measures, evaluate progress.

Revise or Reward

Acknowledge the employee for all progress as soon as possible. Make revisions in your strategy or plan where necessary and implement with the employee's agreement.

The "IMPROVER" Process

Identify the need...	What is the motivator? Is there a problem? Would career coaching be more appropriate?
Map out your strategy...	Write out the approach you will use.
Plan your coaching...	Lay out a plan for your participation and plan the meeting with the employee.
Recommend the actions...	Meet with the employee. Lay out the situation and facts, and your strategy, plan, and recommended actions.
Obtain agreement...	Be sure that everything is aligned upon and agreed to between you and the employee.
View performance...	Observe the employee's performance personally.
Evaluate...	Using the agreed upon measures, evaluate the employee's progress.
Reward or revise...	Acknowledge the employee's progress and make revisions where necessary.

Communication:
The Coach's Main Tool

You are 100% Responsible

" Effective communication is being 100% responsible to ensure that a message is received and recreated"

While you won't find this as a dictionary definition, it turns out to be a useful way to operate with other people. To the extent that you're willing to be completely responsible for making sure that your message is received when you're the one speaking — and; you're willing to be just as responsible to receive someone else's message — you can be an effective communicator. Being effective in this way means that you can get your job done and get the results you want!

Barriers to Effective Communication

A lot of things stand in the way of communicating effectively.

Many people *talk* and then *blame* the other person for not listening. An effective communicator always takes responsibility for both sides of the communication.

Some people have the notion that conversation is communication — they talk *at* each other with neither person hearing what the other is saying. No message gets received on either side and no communication occurs! Again, the process has to do with ensuring that messages are actually received.

The most important thing to remember is that you need to be willing to be 100% responsible to communicate. If you really *want* to get your message across, you will! If you really intend to get the other person's communication, you will! When you are willing to be responsible, you will always find a way to communicate effectively — in every circumstance, regardless of the problems or barriers. That's the secret of true communication.

Listening

Probably the major block to being an effective communicator is your ability (or willingness) to listen — really listen — to what another person is saying. The problem in listening has a lot to do with the fact that most people are distracted and find it difficult to concentrate entirely on the other person. Distraction comes from many sources: noise in the environment, the clutter of papers and unfinished tasks in your office, the press of a busy schedule, and — the strongest of all distractions — the little voice inside your own head.

The Little Voice In Your Head

It's the little voice that is constantly evaluating and judging what other people say, that keeps reminding you that you're hungry, or late, or bored, or not interested, or too busy. Stop for a moment as you read this material and listen to the little voice. What is it saying right now...?

Focusing Your Attention

In order to be a good listener, you have to focus your attention. In addition, if you are concentrating on the person in front of you, you will begin to understand other, more subtle forms of communication including facial expressions and body language. This focused listening will greatly improve your ability as a coach.

Practice... Practice... Practice...!

It may be difficult at first to concentrate and become a focused listener. Practice will sharpen your listening skills and your ability as a coach better than any other thing you can do!

Communication for Results

The main purpose of communication at work is to produce results. In order to be most effective, it is important to understand the various forms of communication and how you can use them to your advantage.

Four Basic Forms

There are four basic and separate forms of communication for results — *declarations, assertions, requests,* and *promises.*

A **declaration** is a statement about the way things are, or the way they are going to be, and is effectively made only by someone with the appropriate authority. Examples of declarations include policies, procedures, mission statements, reporting structures, rules, and regulations.

An **assertion** is a statement in which there is no action expected from the listener and has inherent in it the possibility that the speaker can provide evidence that the statement is true. *"I'm pleased to report that we have met our targets for the second quarter."* A response may be appropriate from the listener such as *"That's great...!"*, but no specific action is called for.

A **request** is a statement (sometimes in the form of a demand) or a question in which a specific action or specific information is expected in return. *"Please have the information to me by Friday."*

A **promise** is a statement in which a specific action is agreed to be completed by a specific time. *"I will have the information to you by Friday." "I'll have the production figures completed by the end of the first week in each quarter."*

Use Communication Effectively

It is important to use declarations, assertions, requests, and promises effectively. If you want to make a request, putting it in the form of an assertion confuses the listener and often leads to a misunderstanding. The assertion: *"This report is not well organized..."* may not produce the specific result you want. A request in the form... *"Please reorganize this report so that there are chapter headings and include a table of contents in the beginning..."* gives the listener a clear and specific action to take. The request can be strengthened by adding a deadline. *"Have the report back to me by Wednesday at noon."*

Actions Take Place in Time

A promise should also be a clear statement of the action to be taken and the deadline to be met. *"I'll put in the chapter headings, add a table of contents, and have the whole thing back to you by Wednesday at noon."* Note that a vague statement of intent is not a promise. *"I'll try to get it done by noon on Wednesday, but I have a pretty busy schedule and it may slide a few days."* You should not be willing to accept this type of low-level communication. Press for a specific promise — clear action — exact time. *"If you can't definitely complete it by Wednesday at noon, when can you be certain to have it?"* *"I'll have it by nine on Friday..."* is a clear promise.

Keep a Record

It is also valuable to keep a record of the promises and requests (including dates) that you make as well as those made by others to you. Such a record allows you to follow up on your own actions and to manage the activities of your subordinates with greater clarity.

By pressing your subordinates (and by being responsible yourself) to: distinguish among assertions, declarations, requests, and promises; make clear requests and promises; and keep a record of requests and promises; you can increase the ability to produce results quickly and easily for both you and your employees.

Dialogues and Discussions

In addition to the four basic forms, communication may be distinguished between dialogues and discussions.

A *dialogue* is an interaction between colleagues where each person comes to the interaction with the intent to discover new possibilities, opportunities, and recognizing that there is greater power in the interaction than can be accomplished individually. There are, however, some basic ground rules necessary for the dialogue to be effective.

- Each person needs to come to the interaction as colleagues, equals. No positionality. Not as boss and subordinate, but as peers working together.

- The participants have to be willing to suspend their assumptions, and pre-concieved notions so that there is the freedom to express ideas, concerns, and thoughts without having to defend or justify. This leaves each person open to discovering existing limitations or barriers brought on by those existing notions.

- Actions may result but that is not the intent. The objective is to open up the subject for exploration and insight.

Positional vs. Non-Positional

In a discussion you are presenting your point of view with the intention of defending it against possible objections or alternative viewpoints. A discussion is positional while the dialogue is non-positional

Given the distinction between these two types of interactions, it becomes clear that the dialogue offers the best situation for interacting about an individual's career.

The discussion, on the other hand, is a good approach for dealing with performance situations. These conversations require you to take a position about the actual performance of the individual and may require you to defend your view and convince the individual of the importance and appropriateness actions you may be proposing.

Using these distinctions regarding your interactions with your employees will give you a better approach to each of the two types of meetings, allowing you to be even more effective.

Communicate to Produce Results

The main purpose of communication at work is to produce results. In order to be most effective, it is important to understand the various forms of communication and how you can use them to your advantage.

Your Current Communication Skill

Are You Meeting Your Own Standards?

Test your ability to be an effective communicator and discover where you can make some needed improvements. Check your answer to each of the questions as honestly and as objectively as possible.

When I communicate, I (Seldom, Sometimes, Often):

	SELDOM	SOMETIMES	OFTEN
1. Talk before I think…	_____	_____	_____
2. Talk more than I listen…	_____	_____	_____
3. Listen more than I talk…	_____	_____	_____
4. Take time to instruct others properly…	_____	_____	_____
5. Look for what's wrong in what others say…	_____	_____	_____
6. Hear the main idea clearly…	_____	_____	_____
7. Pretend to understand when I don't…	_____	_____	_____
8. Encourage feedback and correction…	_____	_____	_____
9. Forget to really acknowledge others for a job well done…	_____	_____	_____
10. Know how to say *no* effectively…	_____	_____	_____
11. Make others still feel OK even when criticized…	_____	_____	_____
12. Try to dominate communications…	_____	_____	_____
13. Forget to say *hello* and establish eye contact…	_____	_____	_____
14. Blame others…	_____	_____	_____

When I communicate, I (Seldom, Sometimes, Often):

	SELDOM	SOMETIMES	OFTEN
15. Miss the point of a statement or question and not ask for clarity...	_____	_____	_____
16. Complain more than come up with positive solutions...	_____	_____	_____
17. Look for and give credit where credit is due...	_____	_____	_____
18. Gossip too much (gossip is telling what is wrong to someone who can't do anything about it)...	_____	_____	_____
19. See the basic good in people and promote that...	_____	_____	_____
20. Seek out new ideas and opinions...	_____	_____	_____
21. Argue frequently...	_____	_____	_____

Go back over the assessment you just completed and select up to five behaviors that you would like to modify. Write them in the spaces below.

Behaviors I would like to modify:

1._____

2._____

3._____

4._____

5._____

The Coaching Meeting

Holding a career management or performance meeting with your employee can be simple and effective if you follow a set of basic rules that will guide you through the meeting.

Desired Outcomes

The desired outcomes from a successful meeting are:

- Employee realizes the reasons for the discussion — organizational as well as personal.

- Employee knows what support is available and how it can be of importance to his or her future.

- Employee knows exactly what the next steps are.

- Employee takes full responsibility for the next steps.

Basic Rules

The basic rules include:

Plan the Meeting

- Know what you want to accomplish yet be open and flexible to what may be needed during the conversation.

- Review any previous meetings to see what happened and determine what may need to be followed up in this meeting.

- Set up your employee to prepare anything you think will be needed for the meeting to be of the greatest benefit for them.

- Prepare an agenda that is flexible yet uses the time effectively. Include all of the points or areas that you need to cover. For performance lay out your agenda following the IMPROVER formula. In a career conversation your agenda needs to be more flexible.

- Eliminate distractions — phone calls and other interruptions.

- Use a suitable location — quiet, uncluttered, comfortable.

- Set aside an appropriate amount of time.

- Review any deficiencies — real or imagined — you think you have that might get in the way?

- Are there any labels, attributions, or characterizations that you have assigned to this person which may be limiting? What evidence do you have that would open possibilities?

- Are you motivated to have the discussion? Does the employee need motivation?

Listen and Communicate Consciously

- Listen carefully. Be honest and direct. If you need to think about the answer — take the time to do so. If you don't know the answer — say so.

- Suspend your assumptions and existing notions so that you can actually hear what they are saying.

- Listen behind what they are saying to see what they need to be supported.

For Career Management Meetings Use the Five Elements

- *Assess* — skills, accomplishments, interests, vision.
- *Investigate* — needs, challenges, opportunities.
- *Match* — assessment with the needs, challenges, opportunities.
- *Choose* — targets of opportunity.
- *Map* — plan with action steps.

For Performance Meetings Use the IMPROVER Process

- *Identify* — the need for performance coaching.
- *Map* — your strategy for improvement.
- *Plan* — your coaching.
- *Recommend* — the actions to be taken.
- *Obtain* — employee's agreement.
- *View* — employee's performance.
- *Evaluate* — ongoing performance.
- *Revise or Reward* — plans and progress.

In the Appendix you will find a series of forms that can be used by both you and your employees to prepare for either a career or performance meeting. Save the blank forms and reproduce them as necessary.

Holding the Career Management Meeting

Career management meetings can be separated into two broad categories — the meeting called by your employee to discuss a specific career management issue or to share his or her plan with you; and the meeting that you call to find out something about your employee's career plans.

Employee Initiative

If the employee initiates the meeting, you need to be prepared to listen and understand clearly before responding in any way. Listen for any indication that the person is stuck in any one of the five elements. Be particularly aware if they haven't clearly expressed their overall vision of their worklife and the contribution they're interested in making to the company. Be sure you have set aside your judgements or characterizations.

Be Clear About The Employee's Vision

Before you get too far into the details of the career plan, be certain that you understand the employee's vision. If not — ask questions. It will be much easier for you to coach the individual if his or her vision is clear to you, because you'll be able to guide the employee in the direction of the vision rather than along some arbitrary path that will lead to something that may not really interest them. For example, the employee may feel that the only way to get to where he or she wants to go is to be promoted. It may be, that what would really put the individual on the right path is a lateral move, or even staying in the current position and developing a new skill.

Reality Testing

When an employee has come in to show you a career plan, your principal coaching role is to provide some reality testing for the plan. Here are the questions you need to ask:

- Are the steps achievable, and will they lead to where the employee really wants to go?

- Is the time frame of the plan realistic?

- Will the earlier steps in the plan give the individual the necessary skills and experience to complete later steps?

- Does the plan have a realistic time frame given the employee's workload, the time required to get the training in each step, and the cost and availability of the training?

- Is the current level of the individual's performance consistent with the overall vision and goals?

- Does the plan include an appropriate list of resources required and questions to be answered?

- Are the needs of the company properly considered?

- Is the plan workable in the environment of the company?

Supporting the Plan

Your role as a coach in this meeting may also have to include suggestions about ways in which you can be in partnership with your subordinate in carrying out the plan. Here are some examples:

- Suggest various forms of on-the-job-training that you could set up for the employee.

- Look at new or expanded responsibilities that you can give the employee to support his or her development.

- Direct the individual to available courses either in or out of the company that would be of help to both of you.

- Be clear that the plan includes specific attention to the employee excelling on the current assignment with you.

Coach's Initiative

When you have called the meeting, and your subordinate does not yet have a career development plan, the first meeting will probably be about starting the process. This meeting should start with your asking them to share with you, informally, where they see their worklife, career, and contribution going with the company. A good opening question might be — *"If you could do anything you wanted in this company, and there were no constraints of any kind, what would you really like to do or be."* By having this discussion, you'll gain valuable insights to the employee's vision as well as demonstrate your caring and willingness to be in partnership with them.

In this or subsequent meetings, you can cover the other issues in the five elements and support the employee in developing a career development plan that is both realistic and satisfying to both of you. The effort and time will contribute significantly to the success of both partners.

Holding the Performance Meeting

Performance meetings are almost always called by you rather than by your employees. It is particularly important that you are well prepared with the evidence that prompted you to call such a meeting. To the extent that your evidence is clear and irrefutable, you will be able to make a strong case for improvement, and your employee is more likely to agree with your remedies, as well as the need for change. It is also important that you refer back to any standards you set with the employee, or any agreements you made about the quality or quantity of his or her performance.

Be Direct

Open the meeting with a direct statement: *"I have not been satisfied with one aspect of your work, and I called this meeting to discuss it with you to work out a way of making some improvements…"* Don't spend any time in informal chit-chat, which only serves to increase the tension. Get right to the point.

Listen Openly

After you have described the situation in detail, give the employee ample opportunity to respond in any way they see fit. While they are responding, maintain your attention and use your best listening skills without judgment or evaluation of what they have to say. Give them the experience that you are interested in what they have to say and are willing to listen. Don't nod your head, or otherwise give any indication that you are in agreement with the individual's position. Remain as neutral as possible.

Maintain Your Position

When they have concluded, you should respond from the point of view of ensuring that the individual understands your position and recognizes the need for the change. If he or she resists your appraisal, you will have to maintain your position and insist on a commitment to improving the performance in question. As a last resort, make it clear to the employee what the potential results could be if the unsatisfactory performance is not corrected to meet your standards.

Finish with Clear Agreements

Be clear about the kinds of actions you would like the employee to take. Whenever possible, give him or her some options. End the meeting with a clear agreement as to the actions that will be taken, when they will be implemented and completed, how you will measure satisfaction, and when the next meeting will be held.

Coaching Scenarios

Practice, Practice, Practice!

The following scenarios are taken from real situations at a wide variety of organizations across the country. You can use them to practice with a colleague, or to prepare for a difficult session that may be approaching. Suggested answers may be found beginning on page 57.

1. You know that you cannot let _____ leave her job; you just spent $10,000 on her training. It's clear that this may not be the perfect job for her. She is unhappy about what she is doing now and has identified another opportunity she'd like to take. You can't afford to lose your investment right now. What do you do?

2. _____ is someone who has been rated outstanding for ten years in a row. He has had experience in a number of staff and line jobs, and is enthusiastic and reliable. He is ready for a change and looking for better self development as well as challenging and satisfying opportunities. How can you keep up his enthusiasm when you know that the chances of vertical promotion are minimal?

3. _____ is a programmer and is tired of doing the job. She has 12 years in the company, most of it in programming, and wants to stay on for security and other personal reasons. You can clearly see that she is stagnating. She is not performing poorly, but you have a strong sense she is doing just enough to hold on. How do you address this?

4. _____ is bright, knowledgeable, ambitious and effective, but has a real superior chip on his shoulder in his communications and his attitude. You can't fault his performance, but you know this attitude will get in the way of his career; and that if he really wants to advance he must work on this issue. How and what can you tell him?

5. _____ has identified Marketing as a department in which she is interested. She doesn't know anyone in that department nor do any of her friends. She comes to talk to you about ways to move closer to that field. What can you tell her?

6. _____ read an article in a recent newsletter about a task force that sounds interesting. He is brand new on his current job, has not yet "proven" himself, and is therefore nervous and reluctant to speak with you about his desire to be on the task force. He brings it up during a casual conversation about how he is doing on the new job. What do you say?

7. _____ is an excellent secretary. She likes her job and doesn't have aspirations to "climb the ladder." However, she feels she needs a change and wants to handle more responsibility on her current assignment. What can you say and do?

8. _____ is an excellent worker looking for promotion, yet makes no attempt to socialize and get to know others, nor do others go out of their way to seek him out. You know he has to take more responsibility for developing his network in order to advance. What do you say?

9. _____ has a very promising future with the organization. You want to support her as much as possible, but if you give her too much praise you will further inflate an ego that may already be an issue. What can you say to her?

10. _____ wants to be a manager, but has no idea whether he would be good at it or not. You are neutral about his ability to be a manager and haven't seen him in action in that role. What can you tell him?

11. _____ was passed up for a promotion and has come to you to complain. You know that there was considerable politics involved, but that she did not network effectively to be seriously in the running. What do you tell her?

12. You offered a promotion to _____ and he came back and said that he didn't think the job was right for him. What do you say?

13. You hear a rumor that _____ is looking around for a new job, but she hasn't told you directly or asked for your advice. You are not willing to lose her suddenly. What can you do?

14. _____ is three years from retirement and has begun to "coast." He has been well respected in the organization for the quality and quantity of his work. You need his continued best effort. What can you say and do?

15. You promoted _____ a year ago, but she hasn't been effective in the new job and should probably go back to where her work was excellent. How do you handle it with her?

16. You have recommended several different training programs to _____ in the last few months, but he has yet to take advantage of any of them. You are anxious for him to develop more rapidly. What can you say?

17. _____ who is normally a good performer has been showing signs of either physical or emotional distress for six weeks and her work has suffered. She has not confided in you, but you are certain that something must be wrong. At the very least, you need to get her work back up to an acceptable standard. What should you say and do?

18. _____ is a good performer, but will never be accepted as a manager unless he handles his wardrobe and personal grooming with more care. How do you approach him and what do you say?

19. In the last meeting you had with _____ she left angry and upset because you expressed your dissatisfaction with her work. She has improved slightly, but not yet to your standard or satisfaction. You would like her to leave the meeting in a more positive state this time. What can you say?

20. Music is _____ favorite thing and he plays in a professional group nights and weekends. Sometimes, his interest in music and his "second career" gets in the way of his getting the job done. What should you do?

21. _____ comes to you more often than necessary for help in solving problems. What can you say to her to have her become more self-reliant without having her leave the meeting feeling she can't use you as a resource any longer?

22. Whenever you talk to _____ about a performance problem, he becomes defensive and blames others for the difficulties. How would you handle this?

23. You have heard about a task force that would be just right for _____. When you tell her about it, she asks if you are trying to get rid of her. You value her ability, and are interested in her development. What do you say?

24. Every time you ask _____ to do a task in a specific way, he argues with you and winds up doing it his own way. How can you handle this?

25. _____ has decided to go back to graduate school full time to get an advanced degree. You cannot afford to lose her and would like to convince her to go to night school, even though it would take twice as long. What can you do and say?

26. Upward mobility in the organization has been severely reduced in recent years and some of your employees are frustrated and angry about what they see as a lack of opportunity. One of your best performers comes and complains—including a thinly veiled threat to leave if he doesn't get promoted soon. What do you say to him?

27. _____ tells you that your job is the only place for her to move up, but she thinks you are going to stay in it for another 20 years. What can you tell her if you plan to stay for a long time? What if your plans include moving, but not for several years?

28. You have reached the point where you are ready to fire _____ if his attitude doesn't improve. You are afraid that there might be an EEO problem if you fire him? What can you do and say?

29. _____ is on a fast track, and needs more experience in other departments. You hate to lose her because she is doing an important job for you. She recognizes the situation in the same way that you do and has come to talk to you about it? How can you support her without undermining your own work?

30. Two of your best employees are highly competitive because they think they are vying for promotions into the same position. You notice that the competition sometimes damages their ability to get a job done together, and diminishes the experience of teamwork for the rest of your group. How can you coach them, both individually and together?

31. Your boss asks you for your opinion of _____ for a promotion to a higher level of responsibility. You really like him, but don't think he is ready for the new responsibility. You don't want to be the one to stand in his way, but you have a responsibility to tell your boss the truth. What do you tell your boss? What do you tell the employee?

Main Points to Remember

- **Career and Performance Management** is the process in which employees take responsibility for developing their ability to make an expanded contribution to the organization; a contribution linking individual work satisfaction and performance to the goals and challenges of the organization.

- **Performing well** in the current job is the foundation upon which future possibility is built.

- The role of the manager is that of a **coach**.

- Coaching is a **partnership** in which it is possible to realize mutual potential.

- Performance coaching requires you to **hold a specific position** with regard to a change in attitude or behavior. Career coaching requires you to **remain as neutral as possible**.

- The blocks that **"DAM"** up your ability to be a good coach...

  Deficiencies ....Real or imagined...knowledge, skills, experience.
  Attributions ....About you, the organization, or others.
  Motivation ....Your own, others.

- **AIM** your employee at **Career Management**...

  Has your employee:

  Assessed ....skills, interests, qualities, experience, strengths, weaknesses/shortcomings, vision?

  Investigated ....needs, challenges, opportunities?

  Matched ....assessment with needs, challenges, opportunities?

  Chosen ....targets of opportunity?

  Managed ....Created and implemented a plan with action steps...skills to develop, behaviors and attitudes to modify, goals to meet, support to enlist?

- **"IMPROVER"** Process

  Identify ....the need.

  Map ....your strategy.

  Plan ....your coaching.

  Recommend ....the actions to your employee.

  Otain ....the employee's agreement.

  View ....the employee's performance

  Evaluate ....the result of the actions taken.

  Reward or Revise as appropriate.

- **Effective Communication** is being 100% responsible to ensure that a message is received and recreated.

Career Assessment

Introduction

The formal purpose of career assessment can be stated as:

> *"Developing a clear understanding of one's natural style, motivation, skills, internal barriers, and developmental needs in relation to work and career."*

There are four basic elements that define who people are in relation to their worklives (see diagram on opposite page):

Style... In what ways do people prefer to relate to the world? How do they *like* to work? What kind of work environment do they prefer? What are their preferred management and/or leadership styles? What are the appropriate contributions for them to make to an organization? How do they relate to people, and around what kinds of bosses and colleagues and subordinates do they work best?

Motivation... What needs, interests, values and beliefs determine what people like to do best? What is most important for them to retain in their worklives? What kind of work do they really want to do, and what is it that they don't want to do? What do they want to *put into* their work and what do they want to *get out of* it?

Skills... What are people able to do? What are the things they can do and would really like to do? What skills can they take with them wherever they go? What skills do they most want to use in their work?

Internal Barriers... People have attitudes and behavior patterns that stand in their way of getting what they want. These internal barriers become easier to deal with when they become consciously apparent.

Developmental Needs

From an understanding of these four elements people are better able to derive their developmental needs. What would they like to be able to do or need to do better or differently, and what's in the way of having that happen and interferes with them making full use of their potential?

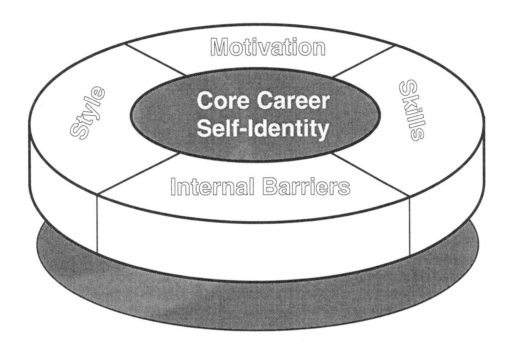

Elements of Effective Career Assessment

Selected References

General Comments

The field of career management contains a large body of knowledge in the form of online resouces, books, papers, magazines, journals, tapes, and other sources of information. The list presented here is only a small portion of the whole, but is useful in providing a supplement to the work you have done in this book. Your local library or, if you are near one, a university library will provide significantly more material if you want to research further.

Internet Resources

Although there are numerous Internet sites providing business information, it is impossible to say with any certainty which ones will survive and which will disappear. Included here is the description of a small number of sites that have been active for three years or more (survivors, by Internet standards). These sites provide useful information about business, industry, economics, and personal or professional development; or they represent doors into a larger set of informative sites.

American Society of Association Executives
http://www.asaenet.org
> A gateway to hundreds of pages of associations in a wide variety of fields. Use this site whenever you need quick information about a new field. Any association's main purpose is to promote its industry, and a conversation with a local association executive can give you vital information and networking contacts.

Big Book http://www.bigbook.com
> Provides "yellow page" listings for more than 16 million U.S. companies, along with information about the company and its location. This site is one of the best business information sources on the Internet. Companies may be selected by category, business name or location.

@brint.com, The Biztech Network http://www.brint.com
> A large source of literature on business and technology including the full text of thousands of articles about the most important business issues of the day.

CEO Express http://www.ceoexpress.com
Provides access to sources of business information through Internet links. Includes links to hundreds of newspapers, business magazines, newsfeeds, business news, technology magazines, custom news and more.

Fast Company http://www.fastcompany.com
One of the best sites for following the changes in the work world. Here's their quote about their mission: "Fast Company aims to be the handbook of the business revolution. We will chronicle the changes under way in how companies create and compete, highlight the new practices shaping how work gets done, showcase teams who are inventing the future and reinventing business. Most of all, we will equip the people exploring this uncharted territory with the tools, techniques, models, and mind-sets they need." They deliver on this goal admirably.

Hoovers Online http://www.hoovers.com
A top site for ongoing research. Track your vendors, clients or competitors. Up-to-date profiles, contacts, news articles, business travel, career center and more. Much information available free, with in-depth data available for nominal membership fees.

Inc. Magazine http://www.inc.com
Inc. provides a compendium of databases on business subjects, along with a search engine for finding specific information.

JIST http://www.jist.com
A catalog of just about every career development and job search book available; a detailed list and description of links to all the best career, job, resume, and education resources; and an excellent jumping off point to the career and job search world. Navigate from the home page through Selected Links to Clearinghouses.

Library of Congress http://lcweb2.loc.gov/catalog
Containing about 18% (almost 5 million records) of the Library of Congress catalog, this database allows you to sort the results of your search by the title of the reference, its publication date, or by its Library of Congress catalog number.

Noble Internet Directory http://www.experts.com
If you need to find an expert in almost any field, here is the place to start. The directory is interactive and global, and can be searched by category, topic or name.

NY Public Library http://gopher.nypl.org/research/sibl/index.html
One of the most important sources of business information, this site is provided by the Science, Industry, and Business branch of the New York Public Library. One of the largest sources of information available on business, industry, and science, this is a critical research site.

People Finder http://www.databaseamerica.com/html/gpfind.htm
Sorted by both names and phone numbers, this huge database will help you to find almost anyone you're looking for.

Vox Pop http://www.voxpop.org
A site that's useful, informative and fun. Full of information about government, particularly in Washington. Find out bills and congressional records and who's voting on what, find your representatives, e-mail senators and congresspeople, search for government agencies, find all kinds of international resources, search for government resources in every state. Link to the Jefferson Project, where you can educate yourself on issues either from the "right" or the "left" point of view, voice opinions, catch up on political cartoons and much more.

Web Virtual Library http://www.vlib.org
A detailed catalog of Internet information resources that has been around long enough to have become very large and comprehensive. Extensive lists of business, industry, science, technology, and cultural resources.

Books

A list of recommended books on all aspects of career and professional development follows, arranged by subject. Books are listed under major subject categories, even if they could apply to more than one. Check other related categories of interest.

Assessment

Career Anchors: Discovering Your Real Values, Schein, Edgar, Pfeiffer & Co., 1993.
> This book provides additional detail and insight on Career Anchors–that combination of values, motivations and skills that defines the self and what one finds rewarding, motivating and satisfying in work.

The Character of Organizations, Bridges, William, Consulting Psychologists Press, 1993.
> Using the typology made familiar in the MBTI, a well known expert extends the work to measuring the TYPE of your organization.

Do What You Are: Discover the Perfect Career for You through the Secrets of Personality Type, Tieger, Paul D. and Barbara Barron-Tieger, Little, Brown and Co., 1995.
> Provides considerable additional material on Work Type. The best of the genre and particularly useful in determining likely lateral moves.

Please Understand Me II: Temperament, Character, Intelligence, Kiersey, David, Prometheus Nemesis Book Co. 1998.
> One of the best and most thorough descriptions of the Myers-Briggs types, this book emphasizes that no one type is better than another. An updated and greatly expanded edition of *Please Understand Me*. Keirsey expanded the MBTI work into "temperaments." A leading edge in typology work.

Type Talk: The 16 Personality Types That Determine How We Live, Love, And Work,
> Kroeger, Otto and Janet M. Thuesen, Delta Publishing, 1989. One of the most readable books on type, for the beginner and the expert. Offers insight into why others behave the way the do, and why you are the person you are—on the job, as a parent, in relationships, and in all aspects of daily life.

Type Talk At Work: The 16 Personality Types that Determine Your Success On The Job, Kroeger, Otto and Janet M. Thuesen, Delacorte Press, 1994.
> Are you an ESTJ? Is your boss an INFP? Learn to use people types for better understanding in the workplace.

Career Management

The Art & Science Of Negotiation, Raiffa, Howard, Belknap Press, 1985.
> Learn the fine arts of negotiation and decision making.

Becoming a Master Student, 9th ed., Ellis, Dave, Houghton Mifflin Company, 2000.
> Do you need to go back to school? The tools you need to be successful at any age in any kind of learning situation. (If you don't need it, get it for your kids!)

The Boundaryless Career, Arthur, Michael B. and Denise M. Rousseau, eds., Oxford University Press, 1996.
> A map of new career forms for people making career choices. as well as for various professionals in human resources, counseling and others.

The Brand You 50: Fifty Ways to Transform Yourself into a Brand that Shouts Distinction, Commitment & Passion, Peters, Tom, Knopf, 1999.
> Tom Peters still has his finger on the pulse of what is needed and wanted in the work world. Get your contribution clarified, and get it visible.

Building Your Field of Dreams, Manin Morrissey, Mary, Bantam, 1997.
> Powerful and practical advice from a spiritual leader on bringing your life dreams into reality.

The Career is Dead, Long Live the Career, Hall, Douglas T., Jossey-Bass Publishers, 1996.
> If we think of a career as a series of lifelong work-related experiences and personal learnings, it will never die.

Career Dynamics: Matching Individual and Organizational Needs, Schein, Edgar, Addison-Wesley Pub. Co., 1978.
> Learn how to get what you need while giving your organization what it needs. An oldie but goodie from the author of *Career Anchors*.

The Career Guide for Creative and Unconventional People, Eikleberry, Carol, Ph.D., Ten Speed Press, 1999.
> Provides assessment tools, real-life success stories, and descriptions of over 200 creative jobs.

Career Survival: Strategic Job and Role Planning, Schein, Edgar H. (MIT), Pfeiffer & Co., 1994.
> Discover the critical elements of your job, and learn to prioritize them.

A Company of One: The Power of Independence in the Workplace, Payne, Tom, Performance Press of Albuquerque, 1993.
> Even the corporate employee or the government bureaucrat has customers. Discover the identity of your personal customers and how to keep them satisfied with their supplier (you).

Creating You and Company: Learn to Think Like the CEO of Your Career, Bridges, William, HarperCollins, 1998.
> Self-assessments and planning advice. A good companion to the concepts and processes in *The Career Challenge*.

Creating Your Future: Five Steps to the Life of Your Dreams, Ellis, Dave, Houghton Mifflin, 1998.
> Commit, create, construct, carry out, and celebrate. A popular lecturer and life coach takes you through the steps of his process.

Don't Stop the Career Clock: Rejecting the Myths of Aging for a New Way to Work in the 21st Century, Harkness, Helen, Davies-Black, 1999.
> Career and management consultant Harkness offers exercises for re-careering; aimed at those who are ready for second and third careers and beyond.

Danger in The Comfort Zone: From Boardroom to Mailroom —How to Break the Entitlement Habit That's Killing American Business, Bardwick, Judith M., AMACOM, 1995.
> The dangers of being too complacent with the status quo.

Empowering Yourself: The Organizational Game Revealed, Coleman, Harvey, Kendall/Hunt Publishing Co., 1996.
> This author, a successful business man, tells you things nobody else will: what really happens at the level you aspire to, and what it's going to cost you (in behavior and personal lifestyle changes) to get there.

Encyclopedia of Associations, 35th ed., Gruber, Katherine, Gale Research Company, 1999.
> Lists tens of thousands of associations by career type. This invaluable resource is a quick connection to people who know everything and everyone in any field in which you are interested. Best accessed in your local or business library.

Getting to Yes: Negotiating Agreement Without Giving In, Fischer, Roger and William Ury, Houghton-Mifflin, 1992.
> Practical, readable, concise guide for negotiating effectively.

Free Agents, Gould, Susan B. et al., Jossey-Bass Publishers, San Francisco, 1997.
> This is one of THE best books for today's workplace. How to grow and prosper in spite of the reality that the new flat organization doesn't support continuous upward mobility.

Halftime: Changing Your Game Plan from Success to Significance, Buford, Bob, Zondervan Publishing House, 1997.
> Don't have a midlife crisis but rather "Halftime", where you reevaluate the first half of your life and build on your strengths for the second.

How to Fireproof Your Career: Survival Strategies for Volatile Times, Baber, Anne and Lynne Waymon, Berkley Books, NY, 1995.
> Most people want to make sure—no matter what happens to their current job—that they can continue to earn a living. This book insists that security can be found right in your own head.

Interview for Success, Krannich, Caryl R., Impact Publishing, 1993.
> Sound advice on building networks, asking and answering questions, conducting information interviews.

The Jist Catalog, Jist, Inc., www. jist.com
> Detailed sourcebook and catalog of career references, job-search materials, videos, assessment tests, career software, and training materials.

Klein's Guide to American Directories, B. Klein Publications.
> A directory of directories designed to aid in locating sources in particular fields or areas of work, with information on over 6,000 other directories. Best accessed in your local or business library.

Learning from other Women: How to Benefit from the Knowledge, Wisdom and Experience of Female Mentors, Duff, Caroline S., AMACOM 1999.
> An expert on workplace gender issues presents inspiring research, directions, and guidelines for accessing one of women's best avenues of support.

Live the Life You Love, Scher, Barbara, Doubleday Dell Publishers, 1997.
If you want your worklife to provide you with more than a paycheck, Scher's books are required reading. Scher is a leader in the make-impossible-dreams-happen field.

Jobshift, Bridges, William, Perseus, 1995.
One of the nation's career experts puts perspective on the changes in the work world as they will affect your career.

Mentoring: The Most Obvious yet Overlooked Key to Achieving More in Life than You Ever Dreamed Possible: A Success Guide for Mentors and Proteges, Wickman, Floyd and Teri Sjodin, Irwin Professional Publications, 1999.
Find a mentor for any area of your life. Includes laws of successful mentoring relationships. Written for both mentor and mentee.

Mentoring: The Tao of Giving and Receiving Wisdom, Chungliang Huang, Al and Jerry Lynch, 1995.
Through parables and metaphors, simple, powerful principles helps one strive for a balanced and humanistic approach to mutual learning.

Mid-Career Tune-Up: 10 New Habits for Keeping Your Edge in Today's Fast-Paced Workplace, Salmon, William A. and Rosemary T. Salmon, AMACOM, 2000.
Aimed at those who could use some good solid training in designing daily actions and using broader thinking to better adapt to today's environment. A workbook that puts ideas into real practice.

New Directions in Career Planning and the Workplace: Practical Strategies for Counselors, Kummerow, Jean M. (ed), Consulting Psychologists Press, 1991.
Useful insights for workers and their managers. (This author also wrote *Worktypes*, based on the Myers-Briggs Type Indicator.)

The New Rules: How to Succeed in Today's Post-Corporate World, Kotter, John P., Free Press, 1995.
Based on research done on Harvard Business School's Class of 1974. Learn from their successes following non-traditional career paths.

The New Perfect Resume, Jackson, Tom, Main Street Books, 1996.
One of the best books in the resume field, both for context and technique. We're biased! Tom Jackson was the founder of **The Career Development Team, Inc**. Updated to include consulting presentations, portfolios, internal resumes and more.

The Overworked American: The Unexpected Decline of Leisure,
Schor, Juliet B., Basic Books, 1993.
> Do you think you're working more now but enjoying it less? You may be right. This book provides some interesting insights and possible solutions.

Register of Corporations, Standard & Poor's.
> Provides information on public companies in the United States. Listings by business names of over 37,000 corporations including the names and titles of officers and directors, sales, number of employees, products, and important telephone numbers. Another library resource.

Six Months Off: How to Plan, Negotiate, and Take the Break You Need . . ., Dlugozima, Hope, Henry Holt, 1996.
> Need some time to get yourself together, rest and recharge, find a new direction? How to find the time, the place, and how to pay for it.

Skills for Success, Scheele, Adele M. PhD., Ballantine Books, 1979.
> First published almost two decades ago, the wisdom in this book is still valid—from identifying the false assumptions that keep you from making progress to choosing the mentor who will help you get ahead.

The Time Bind: When Work Becomes Home and Home Becomes Work,
Russell Hochschild, Arlie, Owl Books, 1998.
> A reality check on work/life balance practices.

Up Is Not the Only Way: A Guide to Developing Workforce Talent,
Kaye, Beverly, Consulting Psychologists Press, 1997.
> You needn't climb the ladder to have a successful and satisfying career. Some terrific ideas on the most effective ways to grow from one of the best-known voices in the career management arena.

We are All Self-Employed: The New Social Contract for Working in a Changing World, Hakim, Cliff, Berrett-Koehler Publishers,1995.
> Even people who work for the world's largest corporations can benefit from considering themselves self-employed. This book describes a new way of thinking that will empower you to take charge and improve the quality of your life.

Change Management

The Art of the Long View: Planning for the Future in an Uncertain World,
Schwartz, Peter, Doubleday, 1996.
> How to develop and use the technique of scenarios for envisioning and planning for the future, by a well-known futurist.

The Dance of Change: The Challenges to Sustaining Momentum in Learning Organizations, Senge, Peter, et al, Currency Doubleday, 1999.
> Management guru and *The Fifth Discipline* author Senge and colleagues present updated information for learning organizations. Contains case studies from major corporations and practices and exercises for teams and individuals.

The Employee Handbook of New Work Habits for a Radically Changing World: 13 Ground Rules for Success in the Information Age, Pritchett, Price, Prichett Publishing Co., 1996
> Thirteen guidelines for dealing with today's reality. No matter what your job, these pithy comments are useful and interesting.

From Chaos to Confidence: Survival Strategies For The New Workplace, Campbell, Susan M., PhD., Simon & Schuster, NY, 1995.
> This book is a self-study course on coping with change—how to stretch your comfort zone and build new capabilities.

Healing the Wounds: Overcoming the Trauma of Layoffs and Revitalizing Downsized Organizations, Noer, David M., Jossey-Bass Publishers, 1995.
> This book is useful for layoff survivors, their managers, and their organizations.

Managing at the Speed of Change: How Resilient Managers Succeed and Prosper Where Others Fail, Conner, Daryl R. Villard Books, 1993.
> Innovation and change management for managers.

The New Modern Times: Factors Reshaping the World of Work, Bills, David B., State University of New York Press, 1995.
> All the background behind the current revolution in the workplace.

Managing Transitions: Making the Most of Change, Bridges,William, Perseus, 1991.
> Directed at managers and employees, a book for those carrying out change. Bridges is a leading author, observer and has influence on career and worklife changes in America.

Pack Your own Parachute: How to Survive Mergers, Takeovers, and other Corporate Disasters, Hirsch, Paul, Addison Wesley Publishing Co., 1987.
> Just what the title says.

A Survival Guide to the Stress of Organizational Change, Pritchett, Price, Pritchett Publishing Co., 1995.
> A thin little book packed with useful ideas and helpful hints for adapting. This is a very prolific author with many useful (and usually inexpensive) books on various business change issues.

Transitions: Making Sense of Life's Changes, Bridges, William, Perseus Press, 1980.
> Creative coping with change in life as well as the workplace—don'tjust survive the turmoil; turn it to your advantage. This one is timeless.

When Giants Learn to Dance: Mastering the Challenge of Strategy, Management, and Careers in the 1990's, Kanter, Rosabeth Moss, Simon & Schuster, NY, 1989.
> An older book, but a classic. Become masters of change rather than victims of it. Security doesn't come from being employed, it comes from being employable.

Communication

Are You Communicating? You Can't Manage Without It, Walton, Donald, McGraw-Hill, 1991.
> Learn to use your communication skills to advantage in the information age.

Communicating at Work, Alessandra, Tony and Phil Hunsaker, Fireside, 1993.
> Use all your senses to make sure you're getting the message— or getting your message across!

Hit the Ground Running: Communicate Your Way to Business Success, Kreuger, Cynthia, Brighton Publications Inc., 1995.
> This is not your typical book on communications skills. Learn how to talk to yourself, present a professional image, and draw on your personal strengths. Handle conflict, be assertive, and negotiate!

How to Prepare, Stage, and Deliver Winning Presentations, Leech, Thomas, AMACOM, 1993.
> Detailed and comprehensive book on making effective presentations.

Listening: The Forgotten Skill, Burley-Allen, Madelyn, John Wiley & Sons, 1995.
> Learning to listen actively may be the most important lesson of communication. Your conversations will never be the same again, and you will get more from every presentation and meeting you attend.

People Skills, Bolton, Robert, Simon &Schuster, 1986.
> Today's workplace is all about people—project teams, workout teams, customer interface. Are your 'people skills' as sharp as they could be? Learn listening, assertion, conflict resolution, and collaborative problem solving.

Sweaty Palms: The Neglected Art of Being Interviewed, Medley, H. Anthony, Ten Speed Press, 1992.
>Covers a wide range of subjects concerning the interviewing process. One of first, and still one of the best books on the subject.

Investigating Future Trends

Blown to Bits: How the New Economics of Information Transforms Strategy, Evans, Philip and Thomas S. Wurster, Harvard Business School Press, 1999.
>Required reading for business leaders and others concerned with the economics of the information age. Even the most focused of business models, the most stable of industries, and the strongest of brands can be demolished by new information technology.

Clicking: 17 Trends That Drive Your Business —And Your Life, Popcorn, Faith and Lys Marigold, Harperbusiness, 1998.
>More on lifestyle trends that will create work possibilities, from the famous forecaster of what will be hot and what will be not.

Competitive Intelligence: Scanning the Global Environment, Salmon, Robert and Yolaine de Linares, Economica, 1999.
>The former VP of L'Oreal and his colleague show how to read trends to determine future opportunities. Important training for both career entrepreneurs and intrepreneurs.

The Dream Society: How the Coming Shift from Information to Imagination will Transform Your Business, Jensen, Rolf, McGraw-Hill, 1999.
>The head of Europe's largest think-tank presents a new view of six future "emotional markets" that are the results of information processes being automated. A unique vision of how products will be developed and sold.

Exploring Your Future: Living, Learning, and Working in the Information Age, Cornish, Edward (ed), World Future Society, 1996.
>This is a collection of articles, originally published in *The Futurist* magazine, dealing with jobs, work, careers, and the technologies that will influence them in the years beyond 2000.

Free Market Fusion: How Entrepreneurs and Nonprofits Create 21st Century Success, Jones, Glenn R, Cyber Publishing Group, 1999.
>Interviews with famous futurists— such as the Tofflers, David Osborne, and more— on the convergence of markets and technologies.

High Tech • High Touch: Technology and Our Search for Meaning,
Naisbitt, John with Nana Naisbitt and Douglas Philips, Broadway Books,
1999.
>   The effects and implications of technology on our everyday life are
>   explored by *Megatrends* author Naisbitt and a group including Swatch
>   CEO Nicholas Hayek, filmaker Ken Burns, and Dr. Andrew Weill.

Signs of the Times: Guidance Into Your Exciting Future, Herman,
Roger E., Oakhill Press, 1999.
>   One hundred of the most current trends affecting work and careers;
>   how to keep up with them and use them to empower your future.

Threshold 2000: Critical Issues and Spiritual Values for a Global Age,
Barney, Gerald O. with Jane Blewett and Kristen R. Barney, CoNexus Press,
1999.
>   The Millennium Institute gives impressive information on the impact of
>   our current business practices on the environment and society. The
>   authors present the opportunity to move toward a more sustainable
>   world.

*Trends 2000: How to Prepare for and Profit from the Changes of the 21st
Century*, Celente, Gerald, Warner Books, 1998.
>   Another look ahead at what the near future might be, and advice for
>   making the best possible personal and professional decisions.

Turbulence! Challenges and Opportunities in the World of Work, Herman,
Roger E., Oak Hill Press, 1995.
>   Planning for the future.

Management & Leadership

*Balancing Act: How Managers Can Integrate Successful Careers and
Fulfilling Personal Lives*, Kofodimos, Joan, Jossey-Bass Publishers, 1993.
>   Defines the necessary personal changes to gain work/life balance and
>   encourage the organizational changes needed to create a supportive
>   workplace.

Becoming a Manager: Mastering a New Identity, Hill, Linda A, Penguin
USA, 1993.
>   Making the transition from 'worker bee' to manager, and the skills
>   you'll need.

Broken Ladders: Managerial Careers in the New Economy, Osterman, Oxford University Press, 1996.
> The number of managers is not declining, in spite of newspaper reports to the contrary. But their work and expectations have changed and new skills are needed.

The Corporate Mystic: A Guidebook for Visionaries with Their Feet on the Ground, Hendricks, Gay and Kate Ludeman, Bantam Books, 1997.
> Two top business consultants take a stand for leadership with vision and integrity. Gay Hendricks is a prolific author with many books that center on the critical elements of communication.

Egos and Eggshells: Managing for Success in Today's Workplace, Robinson, Margot, MA, Stanton & Harper Books, 1993.
> This book has more useful ideas on employee motivation and workplace psychology for managers than its title might suggest.

First, Break All the Rules—What the World's Greatest Managers Do Differently, Buckingham, Marcus and Curt Cottman, Simon & Schuster, May 1999.
> Gathered from the data of 80,000 Gallup interviews, the authors find four consistent practices among managers who have created power ful teams and results.

The Last Word on Power: Reinvention for Leaders and Anyone Who Must Make the Impossible Happen, Goss, Tracy and Betty Sue Flowers, Currency Doubleday, 1995.
> When breakthrough results are called for, and the strategies that have allowed you to win in the past no longer work. Goss and others using the technology she presents have long records of success to support their assertions.

Love and Profit —The Art of Caring Leadership, Autry, James A., Avon, 1992.
> The importance of the human side of being a manager.

Managing a Changing Workforce, Losyk, Bob, Workplace Trends Publishing Company, 1996.
> Demographic changes in the population are resulting in a diverse cultural, ethnic and gender workforce at the same time customers are increasingly demanding. This book shows how to parlay the diversity of the former into satisfaction for the latter.

Managers as Mentors: Building Partnerships for Learning, Bell, Chip R., Berrett-Koehler Pub., 1996.
> The art of passing on your wisdom to others.

Managing in a Time of Great Change, Drucker, Peter F., Plume, 1998.
  Up-to-the-minute advice from the perennial (90-year old) management
  guru. Other titles by this author: *The Post Capitalist Society* and
  Managing for the Future.

Synchronicity: The Inner Path of Leadership, Jaworski, Joseph, and Betty
  Sue Flowers, Berrett-Koehler, 1996.
  The son of a famous father documents his quest for a new paradigm of
  leadership. Powerful business and personal transformation examples
  from a close associate of Peter Senge.

Thinking in the Future Tense: Leadership Skills for a New Age, James,
Jennifer, Simon & Schuster, 1996.
  Advice for managers who need to lose old assumptions, change old
  mindsets, learn faster and work smarter in order to keep up with (or get
  ahead of) the changing times.

*Upsizing the Individual in a Downsized Organization: Managing in the
Wake of Reeingineering, Globalization, and Overwhelming Technological
Change*, Johansen, Robert and Rob Swigart, Addison-Wesley Publishing
Co., 1996.
  Effective management in a time of great change.

Networking

Breakthrough Networking: Building Relationships That Last, Bjorseth,
Liilian D., 1996.
  A practical and easy-to-read "how to" book on enhancing your
  career through word-of-mouth.

*Creating Women's Networks: A How-To Guide for Women and
Companies (Jossey-Bass Business & Management Series)*, Catalyst, Shelia
Wellington, Jossey-Bass Publishers, 1998.
  A 15-year study based on successful women's groups within various
  Fortune 100 companies.This comprehensive manual is filled with
  checklists, charts, breakout points, and first-person suggestions that
  turn the advice into a hands-on program.

*Dynamite Networking for Dynamite Jobs: 101 Interpersonal, Telephone
and Electronic Techniques for Getting Job Leads, Interviews and Offers*,
Krannich, Ronald L., and Caryl Rae Krannich, Impact Publications, 1996.
  This excellent guide from respected authors in the career field is aimed
  primarily at the external job seeker, but easily applies to managing your
  career in your present company. Good tips on electronic networking.

Fifty-Two Ways to Reconnect, Follow-Up and Stay in Touch, When You Don't Have Time to Network, Baber, Anne and Lynne Waymon, Waymon & Associates, 1993.
>Another networking classic from the prolific team of Baber and Waymon.

Is Your 'Net' Working? A Complete Guide to Building Contacts and Career Visibility, Boe, Anne, and Bettie B. Young, John Wiley & Sons, 1989.
>The valuable skills of networking from internationally known trainers.

People Power: 12 Power Principles to Enrich Your Business, Career & Personal Networks, Fisher, Donna, Bard Press, 1995.
>How to build personal networks in the workplace without making it an "extra" to-do. Fisher's accessible and easy approach has proven effective with enthusiastic supporters.

Power Networking: 55 Secrets for Personal & Professional Success, Vilas, Sandy and Donna Fisher, Bard Press, 1992.
>Not just how-to tips, but a context of developing supportive, contributing relationships in all areas of your life. This book got top reviews from readers who applied the concepts.

Power Networking: Using the Contacts You Don't Even Know You Have to Succeed in the Job You Want, Kramer, Marc, Vgm Career Horizons, 1997.
>Especially good for the person who feels networking just isn't their strength, this book lives up to its title for both the experienced and the inexperienced.

Personal & Professional Development

The Adult Years: Mastering the Art of Self-Renewal, Hudson, Frederic M., Jossey-Bass Publishers, 1991.
>Here is a little bit of psychology on the stages of life. (You're not the first person who ever felt this way!)

Advancing Women in Business—The Catalyst Guide: Best Practices from Corporate Leaders (Jossey-Bass Business & Management Series), Catalyst, Jossey-Bass Publishers, 1998.
>Based on research, this book reveals how organizations can attract, retain and promote women.

Artful Work: Awakening Joy, Meaning, and Commitment in the Workplace, Richards, Dick, Berrett-Koehler, 1995.
> An inspiring guide to those who want to bring passion and commitment to their work. Renews the experience of work as creative, participative and purposeful.

The Black Manager: Making It in the Corporate World, Dickens, Floyd, Dickens, Jacqueline B., AMACOM, 1991.
> A classic matter-of-fact guide filled with common sense, strategies, models, and worksheets.

Creative Problem Solving, Noone, Donald J., Ph.D, Barron's Educational Series, 1993.
> This inexpensive little paperback has instructions that actually work, if done diligently, for learning to think out of the box!

Creativity and Innovation for Managers, Clegg, Brian, Butterworth-Heinemann, 1999.
> Just how do you "think out of the box" and apply creative solutions? A practical book for putting creativity into business practice.

The Einstein Factor: A Proven New Method for Increasing Your Intelligence, Wenger, Win, Prima Press, 1996.
> Would you like to become a superstar at something? This is a recipe book for stellar performance, creativity and tapping the unused portion of your brain!

Even Eagles Need a Push: Learning to Soar in a Changing World, McNalley, David, Dell Books, 1994.
> Do you need a push? Even the majestic eagle doesn't fly until mama shoves him out of the nest. You, too, can learn to soar! Wisdom from a popular motivational speaker.

The Fifth Discipline: The Art and Practice of the Learning Organization, Senge, Peter, Doubleday Books, 1994.
> A national bestseller that offers an insightful breakthrough in corporate culture, this book offers transformational shifts in business thought based on principles of science, spiritual wisdom, and psychology.

First Things First: To Live, To Love, To Learn, To Leave a Legacy, Covey, Stephen R., Simon & Schuster, 1994.
> Motivation and direction for getting your priorities straight, from the high priest of personal effectiveness. Choose your priorities, manage your time, balance your life, get results.

Generations at Work: Managing the Clash of Veterans, Boomers, Xers and Nexters in Your Workplace, Zemke, Ron, with Claire Raines and Bob Filipczak, AMACOM, 2000.
> These four generations have different concerns, styles, values and ways of working. Conflicts to avoid, and suggestions for mixing the groups successfully in the workplace.

Get a Life Without Sacrificing Your Career: How to Make More Time for What's Really Important, Booher, Dianna, McGraw Hill, 1996.
> Not time-management in the traditional sense, but a book that questions the assumptions we make about the things we *think* we must do, and presents suggestions for simplifying that which we *really must* do.

Getting It Done, The Transforming Power of Self Dicipline, DuBrin, Andrew J., Peterson's Guides,1995.
> Motivation to DO SOMETHING! This author has written dozens of books on management, leadership, motivation, office politics, and human relations.

Getting Things Done When You Are Not In Charge, Bellman, Geoffrey M., Fireside Press, 1993.
> How to get things done when you have more responsibility than authority. You've got more power than you think!

Getting Unstuck: Breaking Through Your Barriers to Change, Simon, Dr. Sidney B., Warner Books, 1989.
> Are you always complaining about something or other, but never doing anything about it? Read this book!

How to Be Organized in Spite of Yourself: Time and Space Management that Works with Your Personal Style, Schlenger, Sunny and Roberta Roesch, New American Library, 1996.
> Clutter, space and time management for the reluctant (or the organizationally impaired). Ten different systems to match ten different personality types.

The Inner Game of Work, Gallwey, Timothy, Random House, 1999.
> From the master coach and author of *Inner Golf* and *Inner Tennis*, this book takes a revealing look at breaking boundaries in your work.

Leading Consciously: A Pilgrimage Toward Self-Mastery, Chatterjee, Debashis, with foreword by Peter Senge, Butterworth-Heinemann, 1998.
> Chatterjee, an international management trainer and consultant to many top corporations, offers a view on leadership, rooted in both science and timeless practices of awareness.

Learning from Other Women: How to Benefit from the Knowledge, Wisdom, and Experience of Female Mentors, Duff, Carolyn S., AMACOM, 1999.
> A mentoring guide based on the experiences of 200 women. This book breaks through myths and fears and helps women to discover how to reach out and learn from other women at work.

Million Dollar Habits, Ringer, Robert J., Crest, 1991.
> Attitudes and habits for success in business. If you like this book, this author has written several others.

Not Guilty: The Good News About Working Mothers, Holcomb, Betty, Scribner, 1998.
> A well-researched and documented account that focuses on the development of guilt in America's working mothers.

The Path of Least Resistance, Fritz, Robert, with foreword by Peter Senge, Publisher's Group West, 1999.
> This long-time associate of Senge's is the originator of "structural consulting". Fritz explores the way an organization's deep structures support or impede learning and growth, including the effects of different divisions of the organization on each other's success.

Race and Rhetoric: The True State of Race and Gender Relations in Corporate America, Fernandez, John P., and Jules Davis, McGraw-Hill, 1998.
> Fernandez, a pioneer in diversity work in corporate America, surveys 25 years of information and develops insights and possibilities that are transformational in the areas of race and gender.

Scenario Planning: Managing for the Future, Ringland, Gill, with Peter Schwartz, Wiley 1998.
> Scenario planning is an effective technique used by leaders of major corporations for preparing different ways to address the uncertainties of the future. Instructions for creating scenarios for your own future.

The Self-Sabotage Syndrome: Adult Children in the Workplace, Woititz, Janet G., Health Communications, 1989.
> Learn how *not* to do yourself in!

The 7 Habits Of Highly Effective People, Covey, Stephen R., Fireside Press, 1990.
> After priorities are chosen and you know where you want to go, Covey addresses the habits, character, and sense of mission that will help you get there. Ten-year bestseller and counting.

Learning from Other Women: How to Benefit from the Knowledge, Wisdom, and Experience of Female Mentors, Duff, Carolyn S., AMACOM, 1999.
> A mentoring guide based on the experiences of 200 women. This book breaks through myths and fears and helps women to discover how to reach out and learn from other women at work.

Million Dollar Habits, Ringer, Robert J., Crest, 1991.
> Attitudes and habits for success in business. If you like this book, this author has written several others.

Not Guilty: The Good News About Working Mothers, Holcomb, Betty, Scribner, 1998.
> A well-researched and documented account that focuses on the development of guilt in America's working mothers.

The Path of Least Resistance, Fritz, Robert, with foreword by Peter Senge, Publisher's Group West, 1999.
> This long-time associate of Senge's is the originator of "structural consulting". Fritz explores the way an organization's deep structures support or impede learning and growth, including the effects of different divisions of the organization on each other's success.

Race and Rhetoric: The True State of Race and Gender Relations in Corporate America, Fernandez, John P., and Jules Davis, McGraw-Hill, 1998.
> Fernandez, a pioneer in diversity work in corporate America, surveys 25 years of information and develops insights and possibilities that are transformational in the areas of race and gender.

Scenario Planning: Managing for the Future, Ringland, Gill, with Peter Schwartz, Wiley 1998.
> Scenario planning is an effective technique used by leaders of major corporations for preparing different ways to address the uncertainties of the future. Instructions for creating scenarios for your own future.

The Self-Sabotage Syndrome: Adult Children in the Workplace, Woititz, Janet G., Health Communications, 1989.
> Learn how *not* to do yourself in!

The 7 Habits Of Highly Effective People, Covey, Stephen R., Fireside Press, 1990.
> After priorities are chosen and you know where you want to go, Covey addresses the habits, character, and sense of mission that will help you get there. Ten-year bestseller and counting.

Soul in Management: How African-American Managers Thrive in the Competitive Corporate Environment, America, Richard F., Anderson, Bernard E., Citadel Press, 1997.
>*Soul in Management* helps to steer managers in the right direction by dealing with misconceptions about race and corporate life, realities of office politics, mentoring, legal rights and more.

Swim With the Dolphins: How Women Can Succeed in Corporate America on their Own Terms, Smalley, Barbara Steinberg, Connie Brown Glaser, Warner Books, 1996.
>This blueprint for managerial achievement presents techinques for success based on traditional "feminine"assets: nurturing, caring, motivating and other empowering characteristics. Remember—dolphins are the only sea creatures who can take on sharks and win!

Taming the Paper Tiger: Organizing the Paper in Your Life, Hemphill, Barbara, Kiplinger Books, 1997.
>Remember the paperless office? Still drowning in a sea of paper? Get organized!

Think Out of the Box, Vance, Mike and Diane Deacon, Career Press, 1995.
>Stories of creative thinking by many of the innovative giants of the twentieth century, from Thomas Edison to Buckminster Fuller. By a former dean of Disney University.

Time Management for Dummies, Mayer, Jeffery J., IDG Books Worldwide, 1999.
>Like all the other *Dummies* books, this one takes the reader by the hand to lead us through the things we thought were difficult. Work smarter, not harder. He also wrote *Find the Job You've Always Wanted in Half the Time with Half the Effort.*

A Whack on the Side of the Head: How You Can Be More Creative, Von Oech, Roger, Warner Books, 1990.
>A first in the genre of creative thinking, updated in the 90's. This author also wrote the inspirationally titled *A Kick in the Seat of the Pants.*

Women Breaking Through: Overcoming the Final 10 Obstacles at Work, Swiss, Deborah, Petersons Guides, 1996.
>Drawn from a survey of 325 mid and senior-level female managers, this book provides insights and strategies for dealing with barriers to advancement for women in the corporate world.

Working Without A Net: How to Survive and Thrive in Today's High-Risk Business World, Shechtman, Morris R., Prentice Hall, 1994.
>Aimed at managers, but useful for the ambitious, this book provides strategies and rules for successful competition.

Developmental Activities

Employees are very often at a loss when it comes to deciding which specific developmental actions to take. In order to help you make suggestions, we have compiled a list of developmental activities from which employees can choose. We have also provided space at the end of the list for you to add any ideas that come to mind.

The activities suggested here range from very simple ones to complex projects. The appropriate choice is entirely a function of the developmental need and the seriousness of purpose of the employee and his or her career or performance development plan. Your support in helping your employees choose appropriate activities will be important, and we recommend that you read through this list and become familiar with the ideas.

1. Take an internal training course in a technical/functional area you would like to master.

2. Take a degree program in a technical/functional area you would like to master.

3. Study and seek certification in a technical/functional specialty in which you would like to be considered an expert.

4. Do a literature search and read the critical books and papers in a technical/functional area you would like to master.

5. Write an annotated bibliography of resources in a technical/functional specialty in which you would like to be considered an expert.

6. Take an external course from a school, institute, or professional society in a technical/functional area you would like to master.

7. Subscribe to and read the principal journals and periodicals in an area of technical/functional specialty.

8. Read, collect, and organize articles in an area of technical/functional specialty.

9. Join and become active in a professional society.

10. Create an organized file of people in your network including contact dates and information, and a bring-up system.

11. Write and submit a paper for publication in a professional journal.

12. Write and submit a paper for presentation at a professional conference or symposium.

13. Prepare a detailed description of an interesting project to which you contributed and present it to colleagues at an in-house seminar.

14. Develop a professional correspondence in which you share ideas with a counterpart in another company.

15. Develop a mentoring relationship with someone you admire and respect.

16. Become a mentor to a younger or less experienced colleague.

17. Ask your manager to give you an assignment that would really stretch you.

18. Write to a senior executive and make a policy or action recommendation that you have studied and thought through carefully.

19. Design and recruit a task force to solve a problem that has been hanging around for a while.

20. Volunteer for a task force.

21. Volunteer to lead a task force.

22. Write a detailed, long-term career vision.

23. Study ways to use a computer to improve the quality, organize, simplify, or speed-up some aspect of your work.

24. Start reading and develop an annotated collection of books, articles, and other information about your industry.

25. Join and become active in an industry trade organization.

26. Research a specific technical/functional issue or problem of current organizational importance and write a detailed analysis.

27. Do a comprehensive self-assessment of your style, motivation, skills, and internal barriers and get feedback from your manager.

28. Meet with your manager and explore if there is a part of his or her job that you could take responsibility for.

29. Start an internal professional network of colleagues who are doing work similar to yours.

30. Pick a specific personal block that has been troubling you and work on reducing or eliminating it.

31. Take a seminar in personal growth — work on your Self.

32. Develop and use a personal management system that really works for you.

33. Differentiate and get clear about your short-term and long-term priorities.

34. Organize your work in a way that cuts down on non-productive activity.

35. Look for an opportunity to take a bigger risk in some area of your work.

36. Find an opportunity to create a process or procedure that will save the company money.

37. Create a file of external consulting resources in any technical/functional areas in which you are working and evaluate them for future projects.

38. Take the time to clean-up and organize your office for most effective use.

39. Delegate as much as possible.

40. Learn to write concise and precise letters, memos, and reports.

41. Study and clearly identify the direction that technology is expected to take in your business unit (department, division, etc.).

42. Develop a periodic employee survey process in your business unit that provides the kind of information you need to plan ahead to get your job done most effectively.

43. Find out as much as you can about a major competitor to your organization — major customers, how products differ from yours, differences in structure, advertising and marketing, etc.

44. Create and recommend a redesign for your organizational structure that uses "empowered teams."

45. Study and master the relationship between meeting organizational needs in changing environments and specific forms of organizational structure.

46. Take a course, read a book, or otherwise improve your understanding of a business subject outside of your current area of expertise, e.g., economics, accounting, marketing, or strategic planning.

47. Expand your reading in the business press — *Wall Street Journal, Forbes, Harvard Business Review, Business Week, Barron's, Fortune,* etc.

48. Seek an international assignment.

49. Study the language of a country where your business unit does major business.

50. Examine the current applicability of a traditional corporate value.

51. Design and implement a survey that determines what your department's employees want and need in order to be empowered to contribute most effectively to meet your department's goals.

52. Create opportunities to spend time in direct contact with your department's customers.

Please add any additional developmental activities that come to mind:

53. _____

_____

_____

_____

54. _____

_____

_____

_____

55. _____

_____

_____

_____

56. _____

_____

_____

_____

57. _____

_____

_____

_____

Coaching Scenarios
SUGGESTED ANSWERS

The material below provides you with suggested answers to the 31 Coaching Scenarios presented on pages 32 through 35. These answers are not intended as the final word in handling any of these issues. We have only attempted to make what we consider to be a reasonable and effective approach to the situation. You may feel that the answer we have provided would not be appropriate in your culture, or that you would not feel comfortable handling the issue in this way. Use the answers here as a guide to developing an approach that would work for you, and consider each answer as one alternative among many possible ways of handling each question. You may also notice that the same or similar answers appear for different questions. This is perfectly appropriate, and you will begin to observe some patterns as you become familiar with the questions and answers over time.

There are a few general rules that are useful to follow, especially in the difficult cases:

1. Begin by stating the issue as simply and as clearly as possible without emotion or embellishment.

2. Let the employee say everything they need to say about the situation first.

3. Paraphrase what the employee said, to acknowledge the situation and to let them know fully that they were heard in the way they wanted to be heard.

4. Then, present the other side of the issue, or any situational constraints that you want to raise. Be as objective and as factual as possible.

5. Look together for alternatives that would allow for a win-win resolution.

6. Get the person's agreement to any actions you request.

1. You know that you cannot let ____ leave her job; you just spent $10,000 on her training. It's clear that this may not be the perfect job for her. She is unhappy about what she is doing now and has identified another opportunity she'd like to take. You can't afford to lose your investment right now. What do you do?

Acknowledge the situation:

_____, I can see why you have decided that this other opportunity looks much better, and I can understand why you would want to move into that position as fast as you could. Right now, we just made a huge investment in your training to do this job, and I don't have the budget to train another new person.

Let them know you want to try to work out a win/win solution:
Let's see if we can break down some of the components of the job you would like to take and see what those elements are. What most interests you in that job? And what aspects of your current position do you least like? How might we incorporate some of those aspects that you would like to have more of into your present job? How might we restructure the aspects that give you the least satisfaction?

Good, if we could do some of those things, would you be able to see staying in this position for at least a year? Don't forget that your added skills in x, y and z would benefit you in succeeding in your other career goals. I think if we could agree on that, I could support you in going into that next position within a year, and I'll make an effort to give you opportunities to expand the skills that will be most useful to you in that next position.

2. _____ is someone who has been rated outstanding for ten years in a row. He has had experience in a number of staff and line jobs, and is enthusiastic and reliable. He is ready for a change and looking for better self development as well as challenging and satisfying opportunities. How can you keep up his enthusiasm when you know that the chances of vertical promotion are minimal?

Acknowledge the situation:

_____, you've certainly demonstrated that you can take on almost any challenge you want, and I can see that a person of your abilities always needs the next challenge to keep enthusiastic and satisfied.
You are also aware of the fact that due to many factors, there is less opportunity than there used to be for upward movement.

Discuss alternatives for a win/win situation:
What did you uncover in your career development work to be the skills you are most motivated to using and developing in the immediate future?

(Employee responds)

Have you given any thought to a lateral move that would allow you to develop some of those abilities more?

-or-

I think we have several projects in this department that would allow you to use just those skills...

If you were to be able to use more of those abilities, and perhaps even go for some additional outside training in that area, do you see your job satisfaction increasing?

If you do these things (x, y and z). I also think that if something should open up as a vertical move, you would be in an even stronger position to be considered for it than you are now, and I would be glad to support you at that time.

3. _____ is a programmer and is tired of doing the job. She has 12 years in the company, most of it in programming, and wants to stay on for security and other personal reasons. You can clearly see that she is stagnating. She is not performing poorly, but you have a strong sense she is doing just enough to hold on. How do you address this?

Acknowledge the situation:

_____, you've been in the programming area for 12 years now. I can understand how that amount of time in any position without change can lead to boredom. Your work has continued to be acceptable, but it's clear to me that you are not as satisfied as you used to be.

You know that in this era of corporate restructuring the standards have shifted. What used to be all right for average work is no longer all right. Everyone has had to do more with less and discover new ways to be as efficient and productive as possible. When restructurings happen, it is the employees who contribute the most value whose jobs are less at risk. And that doesn't just apply here, but in any company.

Make suggestions for possible solutions.

I have two possible suggestions for you. One is to challenge yourself to look for ways you can re-interest yourself: upgrading your skills, troubleshooting chronic problems, asking co-workers for suggestions for newer innovations. The other suggestion is that you do some career self-assessment. In that way you can look at the overall picture of your skills and perhaps some interests you haven't been using and then we can discuss possible lateral moves into other areas of the company.

4. _____ is bright, knowledgeable, ambitious and effective, but has a real superior chip on his shoulder in his communications and his attitude. You can't fault his performance, but you know this attitude will get in the way of his career; and that if he really wants to advance he must work on this issue. How and what can you tell him?

Acknowledge the person

_____, I know that you are a good performer, and it means a great deal that you can always be counted on to produce results. Am I also correct in thinking that you have ambitions of advancing within the company? Good.

I am also interested in having you obtaining your goals, and for that reason, I want to point out an obstacle that you may not have taken into consideration. There's an element in the way that you communicate to other people that has them assess you as having a superior attitude.

Whether or not you really think of yourself as superior, the way it comes across is that you hold people as less able or capable than yourself, and that attitude alienates others. It will get in your way of getting along with others on a team or of having your subordinates really do their best for you.

(Give very specific examples of communications you've observed, at least 3 or 4. You need to be able to provide ample evidence, because the person often does not see from just one example.

After they have seen the point, make your coaching suggestions.)

I think that your being aware that it is a potential problem is half the battle. Let's look at some of the ways you can work on this issue (take a communication course, have some frank discussions with co-workers, and ask them to tell you when you are appearing to be condescending etc.).

Acknowledge his strengths again.

You really are a superb asset to this department, and with some work on this issue your career goals should be well within your reach.

5. _____ has identified Marketing as a department in which she is interested. She doesn't know anyone in that department nor do any of her friends. She comes to talk to you about ways to move closer to that field. What can you tell her?

I can see that you still have a lot of investigation to do before you can determine whether or not Marketing would be the right area for you.

Have you made up a list of questions of what you would like to ask someone in Marketing in an information meeting?

Review list of questions, or if she hasn't any, give her some guidance on creating such a list.

After you are prepared, discuss it with me, and I'll be glad to call my contacts in Marketing and arrange for an information meeting for you.

---

6. _____ read an article in a recent newsletter about a task force that sounds interesting. He is brand new on his current job, has not yet "proven" himself, and is therefore nervous and reluctant to speak with you about his desire to be on the task force. He brings it up during a casual conversation about how he is doing on the new job. What do you say?

Acknowledge the situation:

I can see that this looks like a great opportunity for you, and I'm glad to see that you're excited to take on that kind of challenge.

What I'd prefer this time around is that you spend some time getting to know this job thoroughly first. In addition to your gaining expertise in this area, spending some time getting to know our overall company better will ultimately benefit you on any task force on which you serve. I'm glad you came to me with the request, and I hope you will continue to do so whenever you see other opportunities. Down the road there are bound to be many others and at the right time I'll be glad to support you.

---

7. _____ is an excellent secretary. She likes her job and doesn't have aspirations to "climb the ladder." However, she feels she needs a change and wants to handle more responsibility on her current assignment. What can you say and do?

Acknowledge situation and acknowledge the person.

_____, first of all, I'm really glad you came to me with this. You know I depend on you, and I'm completely lost on the days when you're not around! It's important to me too that you are challenged and satisfied in your position.

First, are there any particular areas of responsibility you've already seen that interest you? *(If so, discuss what skill upgrades might be needed in order to take over those duties, e.g., learning a page layout program to do presentation preparations)*

If person has no idea of what would be next for them:
a. You can suggest some career development work to determine which of their strengths they would be most motivated to develop, and look for possible applications within the job, or
b. you can determine what part of your job you could have better support in and what would be necessary for that employee to develop to take over some of those responsibilities, and you could agree to discuss it again in a few days after you've had time to consider it.

---

8. _____ *is an excellent worker looking for promotion, yet makes no attempt to socialize and get to know others, nor do others go out of their way to seek him out. You know he has to take more responsibility for developing his network in order to advance. What do you say?*

Acknowledge the situation:

_____, I want you to know that I'm really pleased with your performance, and I think that you are doing an excellent job. I'm interested in you furthering your career here, as I know you are.

I know that you like to work on your own, and that you get your best work done in private. But one of the aspects of moving up, both in terms of attaining a higher position and in being successful at it once you get there, is the ability to make yourself known and establish networks of contacts within this department and within the company at large. Do you know why this would be important? *(Discuss).*

Discuss ways to address the situation:
What are some of the situations you could use to begin to widen your network? *(Making a point of going to lunch with coworkers, volunteering for a team project, etc. Discuss options and let employee choose the most comfortable ones.)*

---

9. _____ *has a very promising future with the organization. You want to support her as much as possible, but if you give her too much praise you will further inflate an ego that may already be an issue. What can you say to her?*

Acknowledge the situation by telling the truth:

_____, you did a fantastic job on this project, and I'd like to make a big deal over how great it is, but I notice that I'm reluctant to, and I want to tell you why.

You are clearly someone who excels in most areas in which you endeavor, and I'm also aware that you know that about yourself. What I have picked up on, both on my own and from other people, is that your self-confidence, which serves you very well, can also come across as superiority, which doesn't serve you well. Other people with whom you have to work may feel condescended to and will come to resent it. I'm concerned about a potentially brilliant career being sidetracked by a personality issue that can be easily remedied by bringing it to your attention.

Offer a course of action and your support:
What I'm asking you to do is to be aware of your public identity within the department and the organization as a whole. You may want to ask some other people for validating feedback on this issue. I find that if you are honest and direct about asking people, they'll tell you the truth. I'd be glad to work with you on this, and urge you to talk to me more about it if it's not clear to you.

Acknowledge the person again:
Don't take what I'm saying to mean anything negative about your work, or let it undermine your self-confidence. As always, your work is outstanding. and your confidence allows you to take on big challenges. But what allows people to be successful in an organization as they move on in addition to their work is their ability to interact with others, and I really want to support you in this.

---

10. _____ wants to be a manager, but has no idea whether he would be good at it or not. You are neutral about his ability to be a manager and haven't seen him in action in that role. What can you tell him?

_____, since neither of us is sure how you'd do in that role, I'd like to give you an opportunity to find out. First, I recommend that you do some skills assessment to see if you are even oriented in the direction to really manage people. Secondly, we can work out some opportunities for you to do some supervisory-related activities, such as running a meeting, planning out some projects, etc., that would enable you to start sharpening your managerial skills. I'll check in with you along the way, and we'll see how things are going, and get you the experience you need to determine if this really is right for you.

11. _____ was passed up for a promotion and has come to you to complain. You know that there was considerable politics involved, but that she did not network effectively to be seriously in the running. What do you tell her?

Acknowledge the situation:

_____, I know there must have been real disappointment for you in not getting the position. (Allow her to respond and express any upset and emotions.)

One of the facts of organizational life is that in order to have things happen the way you want them to happen, it's often not what you know but who you know. Making yourself known to key players is an important part of your ongoing career development. Do you feel that you handled your networking with people to the best of your ability? (Discuss the particulars of the situation, and point out where other opportunities may have been missed.)

Offer your support for the future:

Why don't you think about some ways you could increase your exposure to the people you will need to be known by, and discuss them with me. Let's start working on it now, so that the next time an opportunity arises, you are in a better position to have what you want happen.

12. You offered a promotion to _____ and he came back and said that he didn't think the job was right for him. What do you say?

Acknowledge the situation:

_____, I'm surprised that you don't want this opportunity. I'd like to know some of the thinking behind your decision. Exactly what aspects of the job aren't right for you? Do you have other goals of which I'm unaware?

Listen to find out if the decision is based on clear self-knowledge of career goals, strengths and direction, or if what was underlying it was simply fears of not being successful, or unrealistic illusions about other opportunities for which he is ill-prepared..

13. You hear a rumor that _____ is looking around for a new job, but she hasn't told you directly or asked for your advice. You are not willing to lose her suddenly. What can you do?

Acknowledge the situation:

_____, I've heard some rumors that you're thinking of moving into another position. Is this true? I would be sorry to lose you, and I'm very interested in keeping you in this department. What are the factors motivating you to search elsewhere?

Explore the reasons, identify the chief motivators for her desire to move, and discuss possible alternatives for a win/win situation:

You're a valuable contributor, and your work has always been excellent. If we were able to work out some opportunities for you to use more of the abilities you want to use right here, would that make a difference in your decision?

If so, make a plan for when you can have another discussion about how to implement the suggestions.

---

14. _____ *is three years from retirement and has begun to "coast." He has been well respected in the organization for the quality and quantity of his work. You need his continued best effort. What can you say and do?*

Acknowledge the situation:

_____, you've been a highly respected contributor for all the years you've worked here. I want to talk to you about the time you have remaining here before you retire. When retirement comes into view, there are a few ways things can go. There's an opportunity to wait out the time, or there's an opportunity to see how you can use the next three years to really leave a "legacy" - perhaps a project that will have real impact, or maybe the coaching of some junior employees who could really use a good mentor. I'd like you to think about what would really stimulate you to keep contributing at the high level you always have, and provide an adequate challenge to keep you interested and satisfied. Think about it and let's discuss some options.

---

15. *You promoted _____ a year ago, but she hasn't been effective in the new job and should probably go back to where her work was excellent. How do you handle it with her?*

Find out how _____ thinks it's going:

_____, you've been in the new position for a year now. I want to take this time to do a review of how things have been going. How do you see your performance in this position versus your performance as a salesperson?

Most people are very aware of when they are not doing well. Allow adequate time for a discussion of what factors the employee may perceive as having been outside constraints inhibiting their success, as well as any personal feelings about the situation.

In terms of career satisfaction, "up" is not the only way. Sometimes what looked like a good idea at the time is a mistake, because it takes you away from doing what you do best. It happens a lot in sales, and in jobs like lab work, where good scientists are promoted to management and no longer are able to do the thing they loved which is research. Ultimately, what is important is that you experience being successful at what you do, and it's clear that hasn't been happening here. For your benefit and the department's, I'd like you to consider whether you'd be happier if you went back to full-time sales.

16. You have recommended several different training programs to _____ in the last few months, but he has yet to take advantage of any of them. You are anxious for him to develop more rapidly. What can you say?

Acknowledge the situation:

_____, over the past months, I've made several recommendations to you regarding improving your skills. You haven't taken any of the classes I've offered to send you to, and it concerns me. Can you tell me why you haven't followed through?

Answer will probably be some form of "not having the time" — which is an indication of not seeing the forest for the trees.
I understand that just getting your scheduled work accomplished takes all of your time and that you are focused on getting the job done. However, when I make a request for you to go to training, I am looking at the future, both for you and for the department. Taking these trainings would facilitate you to get the job done even better and faster. These courses would not only benefit your work here, but would also benefit you directly by adding to your skills for your own future. Do you see the value I'm talking about? Good. I want you to look at the courses and begin to schedule yourself into them.

17. _____, who is normally a good performer, has been showing signs of either physical or emotional distress for six weeks and her work has suffered. She has not confided in you but you are certain that something must be wrong. At the very least, you need to get her work back up to an acceptable standard. What should you say and do?

Acknowledge the situation:

_____, I'm concerned about you. Lately you've seemed tense and upset, and it's taking it's toll on your work. I don't want to pry into your personal affairs if you don't want to talk about it, but is everything all right?

More often than not, people will welcome the opportunity to talk about what's bothering them. They may have been afraid to bring it up themselves. Give her time to tell you what's wrong. Then offer whatever support is appropriate:

_____, what support do you need in order to get things straightened out so that you are able to concentrate on your work again?

If she declines to talk about it, you can say:

_____, it's your privilege to keep your personal matters private. But I have to point out that it's affecting your work, and I need you to be performing at a better level. I'm available to support you in whatever ways I can, and if you change your mind about talking about it, please come see me.

18. _____ is a good performer, but will never be accepted as a manager unless he handles his wardrobe and personal grooming with more care. How do you approach him and what do you say?

Acknowledge the situation:

_____, I want to talk to you about your career development. You're a good performer, and I'd like to see you advance to becoming a manager. But at the managerial level, the stakes are higher in more areas than just your work. One of those areas is personal appearance. You don't want to put any distractions between you and people who need to listen to you, and how you dress and other aspects like your hair, etc., all have an impact on your personal presentation. Whether we like it or not, and whether it should be this way or not, the fact is that personal appearance is a factor in one's career opportunities, and I wouldn't want to see you miss out on good opportunities for you because of this issue.

Continue by making direct suggestions, or by asking the employee who he knows who could help him with his professional image.

19. In the last meeting you had with _____, she left angry and upset because you expressed your dissatisfaction with her work. She has improved slightly, but not yet to your standard or satisfaction. You would like her to leave the meeting in a more positive state this time. What can you say?

Focus on what she has accomplished:

_____, I'm really pleased that after our last conversation you've made a substantial effort to turn things around. I appreciate what you've undertaken, and I can already see the results. There's more to go, but you've made a great start, and I want to support you in continuing in the direction you've been going.

Make some specific suggestions and be sure to get her agreement on any course of action that would be appropriate. Close by thanking her again for making good movement in the right direction.

20. Music is ____favorite thing and he plays in professional group nights and weekends. Sometimes, his interest in music and his "second career" gets in the way of his getting the job done. What should you do?

Acknowledge the situation:

_____, everyone has outside interests besides work, and after work your time is your own. I know music is very important to you, and that's fine, but there are times when your evening hours take their toll in a way that shows up in the quality of your work. Do you know what I'm referring to?

Give examples if necessary.
I have no issue with your outside interests as long as they don't affect the job you do here. I'd like you to think about it and let me know how you can manage it so that the two are no longer in conflict.

21._____comes to you more often than necessary for help in solving problems. What can you say to her to have her become more self-reliant without having her leave the meeting feeling she can't use you as a resource any longer?

_____, I'm glad that you come to me regularly for assistance, because it keeps us in communication about what is going on, and that's important. At this point, though, I think there are some areas where you are ready to make certain decisions on your own. *(Review specifically what some of those areas may be)*. I want you to give it a try for a while and see how it goes. It's okay if you make mistakes, we can tackle those if they come up. But I really think you'll do fine. Let's set up a meeting to review how things are going next week. And don't be afraid to ask me anything that you really need help with before then.

22. Whenever you talk to _____about a performance problem, he becomes defensive and blames others for the difficulties. How would you handle this?

Acknowledge the situation:

It's true at different times and in different situations that others are at fault, or the circumstances can add a lot of constraints that make getting things done the way you want them done difficult.

The important question in any circumstance is what can you do about that situation? You really can't change anyone else. The only place you can look is at how you can act differently to get the outcome that is needed. You need to ask yourself: "How can I respond better? What would I have to change to be more effective?"

23. You have heard about a task force that would be just right for ____. When you tell her about it, she asks if you are trying to get rid of her. You value her ability, and are interested in her development. What do you say?

_____, I'm not trying to get rid of you. In fact, this is just the opposite. I hold your work in high regard, and as such, I'm looking for opportunities that will advance your career. I see this as one of those opportunities that will not only give you an opportunity to shine, but also will increase your skills and at least as importantly, your exposure to other areas of the company that will broaden your perspective and make you that much more valuable. It will also make you known to others who could be important to network with in the future. How do you feel about it now?

24. Every time you ask____to do a task in a specific way, he argues with you and winds up doing it his own way. How can you handle this?

_____, you are clearly a bright individual who has good ideas about the way things should be done. I, too, have ideas, and frankly, I feel like I'm fighting with you all the time. What's more, after we argue, my instructions still aren't followed. I'd like to be able to shift things so that we can discuss your suggestions, and then once the method is decided upon, I can count on things coming back in that same way. I'm willing to listen to your ideas, and implement them when appropriate. And things will not go your way all the time. What do you have to do in order to shift things so that we're working more as partners, and so that I can count on the way things will get done in the end?

25._____ has decided to go back to graduate school full to time to get an advanced degree. You cannot afford to lose her and would like to convince her to go to night school, even though it would take twice as long. What can you do and say?

After you discuss the possible advantages to your preference, such as company tuition reimbursement programs, etc., if she is set on going, you can make a request:

_____, you've given this a lot of thought, and it's an undertaking that's going to effect a big life change for you. I admire you for going for what you really want, and I wish you the best of luck. Of course, your decision also affects this department, and I'm honestly very disappointed to have to lose you! My request is that you take the opportunity to launch yourself in your new venture by leaving here in a powerful way—that means, cleaning up the details of all the projects you are working on, and preparing full instructions for whomever is going to be picking up the projects that will not be complete at the time you leave. I would also like you to help look for and train your replacement—someone who will do the job as well as or better than you! Then, when you leave, we'll all be left looking to the future in a way that's satisfying.

---

26. Upward mobility in the organization has been severely reduced in recent years and some of your employees are frustrated and angry about what they see as a lack of opportunity. One of your best performers comes and complains —including a thinly veiled threat to leave if he doesn't get promoted soon. What do you say to him?

_____, I know that the situation has been extremely frustrating, especially to someone with your abilities. In this situation, you need to take into account the bigger picture of what's going on economically in out company, our industry, and in business in America in general. The blunt truth is that in an era of streamlining and restructuring, there is a definite decrease in opportunities for upward mobility. The factor I ask you to look at which you may not have considered is what's behind your desire for a promotion. There are many times when people confuse promotion with job satisfaction. It may be that you desire to move up, and if you truly do, it's a valid career goal. But if part of what you want is to expand your satisfaction and use more of your abilities, I recommend that you do some career development work. By identifying your skills, values, motivations, interests, etc., and looking at other ways they can be used within the company, you may find that a change of projects or areas may be what you need to keep you satisfied. If, after exploring those options you determine that what you really want is upward mobility, you have a choice. You can do everything you can to see that you are situated in the best position for when things do open up, or you may need to look at moving to another company or even another industry where there is more growth and rapid advancement.

27. _____ tells you that your job is the only place for her to move up, but she thinks you are going to stay in it for another 20 years. What can you tell her if you plan to stay for a long time? What if your plans include moving, but not for several years?

Acknowledge the situation:
I can understand your frustration. It looks as if I am in your way of moving up in the organization. Let's explore if there are alternative ways for you to get what you want.

Look at the possibilities of moving laterally into a department that presents more opportunity for moving up. Look also at the options for lateral moves that might bring more responsibility or more challenging assignments, if not a bigger title. Explore ways of expanding the job she is in under you that will provide her with a more satisfying worklife. If you are planning to move on yourself in several years, share your plans with her (if appropriate to do so) and support her to develop herself toward being your successor.

28. You have reached the point where you are ready to fire __ if his attitude doesn't improve. You are afraid that there might be an EEO problem if you fire him. What can you do and say?

First, discuss the issue with the EEO officer in your organization. As soon as you realize you might have to fire this person, keep careful written documentation of your meetings, your problems with his performance, requests for remediation, his response to your requests, and any other discussions you have or have had in the past. When you are fully prepared, have a meeting with the individual and in your conversation, stick to the documented performance-related facts, and don't get pulled into any other issues. Keep coming back to the documented facts.

29. _____ is on a fast track and needs more experience in other departments. You hate to lose her because she is doing an important job for you. She recognizes the situation in the same way that you do and has come to talk to you about it. How can you support her without undermining you own work?

Again, if all else fails, refer to the answer to role-play number 25. If someone has to leave, get their support in finding and training a replacement in a way that will leave the job in better shape than they found it - ensuring a smooth transition, and an opportunity for everyone to be satisfied.

30. *Two of your best employees are highly competitive because they think they are vying for promotions into the same position. You notice that the competition sometimes damages their ability to get a job done together, and diminishes the experience of teamwork for the rest of your group. How can you coach them, both individually and together?*

_____, I am aware that both you and _____ are looking at the same position, and that you feel as though you are in competition for that slot. You are both excellent performers, and I'm glad to see that you have goals for yourselves. However, the friction between you has been felt by everyone around.

One important aspect of being a leader is being able to work effectively on a team or with a team of people under you. It will be damaging to your future opportunities if you can't demonstrate that ability.

I also want you to note that you are both thinking from a very limited sense of possibilities, focused on only one potential slot in one department. It would be advisable for both of you to do some career development planning, so that you get a sense of the broadest range of possibilities available to you.

31. *Your boss asks you for your opinion of _____ for a promotion to a higher level of responsibility. You really like him, but don't think he is ready for the new responsibility. You don't want to be the one to stand in his way, but you have a responsibility to tell your boss the truth. What do you tell your boss? What do you tell the employee?*

Tell your boss the truth!

I think that _____ is an outstanding performer, and I really like him, but I don't think he is ready for the position yet. I feel that he needs more development in some specific areas and would be willing to support him to create a development plan with a realistic timeline that would allow him to move into the new spot as soon as he is ready.

Tell the employee the same thing.

Appendix

Note: We recommend that you reproduce as many copies of these work sheets as you need. Save the blank forms in this book for further reproduction.

Label Work Sheet

Limiting Label _____

Specific Evidence: **Developmental Opportunities:**

1. _____   1. _____
   _____   _____
   _____   _____
   _____   _____
   _____   _____

2. _____   2. _____
   _____   _____
   _____   _____
   _____   _____
   _____   _____

3. _____   3. _____
   _____   _____
   _____   _____
   _____   _____
   _____   _____

4. _____   4. _____
   _____   _____
   _____   _____
   _____   _____
   _____   _____

5. _____   5. _____
   _____   _____
   _____   _____
   _____   _____

6. _____   6. _____
   _____   _____
   _____   _____
   _____   _____

Situation Work Sheet - Career Management

Think of one of your subordinates who you feel could benefit from a career coaching session, then complete this work sheet.

- Describe the person's current job responsibilities:

- How long has he/she been with the company?

- How long has he/she been in the current position?

- What are the career aspirations of this employee?

- In what element of the career management process is he/she engaged?

- What is the purpose and desired outcome to be produced from your next career coaching discussion?

- Given this employee's aspirations, what are the issues that need to be brought up in your next discussion? Include whether he/she or you have raised the issues involved:

Planning Work Sheet for
Career Management Coaching

Use this worksheet to plan your career management meeting. Bring it into the meeting with you and use it to help create an effective session. Use this form only as a guideline. Remember that the meeting should be a dialogue with your employee. Save the worksheet as a record of your meeting and to assist you in preparing for the next meeting.

Employee Name _____ **Meeting Date** _____

Has the employee been given the preparation sheet and any other information they need so that they are prepared?

YES ❑   NO ❑

Is there anything you would like to say at the beginning of the meeting to acknowledge the employee, or express your gratitude, that would allow them to feel appreciated and in relationship and partnership with you?

What is the starting point for this meeting and what do you see could be accomplished? (Which element are they in and what is the next outcome or step to take?)

What would you like to find out from this employee?

Planning Work Sheet for Career Management Coaching (continued)

What personal development recommendations do you have given their goals, targets, plans and vision? (Skills, Attitudes or Behaviors, Current Job Performance)

What feedback, input or suggestions do you have on their current career plan?

Notes from this meeting:

REMEMBER, THIS IS AN ONGOING CONVERSATION.
IS YOUR NEXT MEETING SCHEDULED? DATE:_____

Employee Preparation Work Sheet

- What are your career aspirations overall or what are your goals for your work life?

- What would you like to be doing 3-5 years from now in the company?

- What do you see as your next move within the company?

- If you want to continue in your current position for the forseeable future, what are some areas that you would like to develop to stay current and valuable in your position?

Employee Preparation Work Sheet (continued)

- What are some areas you would like to strengthen, relative to your current job?

- What are the things you enjoy about your current job or work in general?

- What are the things you like the least about your current job or work in general?

- What support, direction or guidance would you like?

- What questions would you like to ask regarding your career, the company, or your current job?

Situation Work Sheet - Performance

Think of one of your subordinates where you feel performance coaching is needed. Then complete this work sheet.

- Describe the person's current job responsibilities:

- How long has he/she been with the company?

- How long has he/she been in the current position?

- What are the measurable or observable standards for performance in the job?

- Describe the circumstances and what you would like to accomplish from this discussion.

Planning Work Sheet for Performance Coaching

Use this worksheet to plan your performance coaching meeting. Bring it into the meeting with you and use it to help create an effective session. Use this form only as a guideline. Remember that the meeting should be a dialogue with your employee. Save the worksheet as a record of your meeting and to assist you in preparing for the next meeting.

Employee Name _____ **Meeting Date** _____

- Describe in detail, using specific examples, the need for this coaching session:

- What is your strategy for dealing with this situation? (Remember that a strategy is the approach you are going to use, e.g., training, job restructure, relocation, etc.)

Planning Work Sheet for Performance Coaching (continued)

- What are the recommended actions to be taken? (Include a timeline for implementation and check off when the employee agrees.)

_____ ❑

_____ ❑

_____ ❑

_____ ❑

_____ ❑

_____ ❑

_____ ❑

_____ ❑

_____ ❑

_____ ❑

- If this is a poor performance issue, what are the consequences of a lack of improvement?

- Are you certain the employee understands the consequences? YES ❑ NO ❑

- If no, what are you going to do to be sure that the consequences are clear and understood?

Planning Work Sheet for Performance Coaching (continued)

- What is the proceedure or plan for viewing this employee's performance from this point forward?

- What is the date for meeting again to re-evaluate performance?

- Use this section to debrief the meeting. Make note of your impressions and anything that will be of importance or assistance in dealing with this person in the future.

Role Play Work Sheet

Think of a real career management or performance situation you have with one of your employees and write out the situation. Give as much detail as necessary to allow for an effective role play.

_____

_____

_____

_____

_____

_____

_____

_____

_____

_____

_____

_____

_____

_____

_____

_____

_____

_____

_____

_____

_____

_____

Coaching Skills Assessment Feedback

Please check your best observation of your manager with regard to his or her ability to provide effective coaching to you and your colleagues. Be as objective and honest as possible in your assessment. All results are strictly confidential.

Does your manager (Seldom, Sometimes, Often):

	SELDOM	SOMETIMES	OFTEN
1. Listen carefully to what employees have to say?	_____	_____	_____
2. Acknowledge employees when they have accomplished something, even if it seems like a small win?	_____	_____	_____
3. Keep up-to-date about what's going on in the company and provide useful information to employees?	_____	_____	_____
4. Avoid gossiping about employees and maintain confidentiality in discussions with them and about them?	_____	_____	_____
5. Set clear standards of performance and communicate them clearly and as often as necessary?	_____	_____	_____
6. Work and act in a way that sets an appropriate and strong example to employees?	_____	_____	_____
7. Avoid negative comments about the company except when presenting solutions to someone who can do something about it?	_____	_____	_____
8. Earn trust rather than demand it?	_____	_____	_____
9. Confront unpleasant issues when necessary?	_____	_____	_____
10. Keep current about available training and educational opportunities?	_____	_____	_____
11. Make time for employees even when extremely busy?	_____	_____	_____
12. Provide performance feedback as frequently as necessary?	_____	_____	_____

Coaching Skills Assessment Feedback (continued)

Does your manager (Seldom, Sometimes, Often):

	SELDOM	SOMETIMES	OFTEN

13. Seek to find out what may be troubling an employee whose behavior or attitude suddenly changes?

14. Take a real interest in the personal and career growth of employees?

15. Continue coaching employees through difficult times?

16. Look for what works best about an individual and try to support that?

17. Know when to say? *"I don't know"?*

18. Support self-esteem of employees and avoid putting people down?

19. Reach out to employees rather than always wait for them to initiate a discussion?

20. Feel comfortable coaching?

21. Encourage appropriate risk-taking?

22. Maintain a sense of humor?

23. Support employees to network and increase their visibility?

24. Avoid allowing personal prejudice to stand in the way of maintaining a supportive role?

25. Avoid all forms of sexual harrassment and maintain vigilance for self and others?

26. Encourage individual responsibility for career and performance management?

27. Seek professional help when a situation requires it?

Coaching Skills Assessment Feedback (continued)

Does your manager (Seldom, Sometimes, Often):

	SELDOM	SOMETIMES	OFTEN
28. Know when to say *"No"*?	____	____	____
29. Take risks in order to develop people?	____	____	____
30. Let a good person leave if it was in their best interest?	____	____	____
31. Keep current in the industry and share knowledge with others?	____	____	____
32. Give new employees reasonable training and time to learn?	____	____	____
33. Continue personally to seek development and opportunities to grow?	____	____	____
34. Avoid all forms of discrimination and maintain vigilance for myself and others?	____	____	____
35. Confront disruptive behavior quickly and decisively?	____	____	____
36. Do formal performance appraisals at least annually?	____	____	____
37. Discuss career goals and development with each employee at least annually?	____	____	____
38. Consider it more important to be effective than to be well-liked or popular?	____	____	____
39. Have a career plan, keep it current, and work to implement the actions?	____	____	____
40. Provide a proper environment for performance or career development meetings with employees?	____	____	____

When you have completed this form, please return it to your manager. This assessment should be treated with complete confidentiality.

OPTIONAL

_____   _____